No More Salt for Tears

B.L Blocher

Copyright © 2024 B.L. Blocher

All rights reserved. No part of this book may be reproduced or transmitted in any form or by any means, electronic or mechanical, including photocopying, recording or by any information storage and retrieval system without permission in writing from the publisher.

The Emerald City Press— Southington, CT
ISBN: 978-1-7374610-3-6
Library of Congress Control Number: 2024924578
Title: *No More Salt for Tears*
Author: B.L. Blocher
Digital distribution | 2024
Paperback | 2024

This is a tragic account of the authentic story of my mother's childhood in Poland during WWII and the Holocaust.

There is limited fictional dialogue and some events that are woven in to lend continuity to her story. However, everything that I write about regarding what my mother experienced in the ghetto, the concentration camps and the Nazi's and their collaborators is factual and it horrifically happened to her.

Thewatchmaker1939@gmail.com

Dedication

To my mother, Rochela (Bolber) Blocher.

During your time in the concentration camps, you never lost your courage, dignity or self-respect. They took everything else, but they couldn't take that from you…. I'm so proud to be your son.

Introduction

On February 8, 1998 my Mother Rochela (Bolber) Blocher sat down in her home with a film crew from the Steven Spielberg Shoah foundation. The foundation's purpose was to film and document Holocaust survivors' testimonials to be compiled and archived so their stories would be preserved for future generations.

It was an opportunity for my mother to make a first-hand video account of her harrowing experience during her time as a teenager, living in Poland, and surviving the Holocaust.

It was the first time ever that she completely revealed her horrifying journey, from being a carefree little girl living in Vilnius, Poland, to suddenly being targeted and persecuted by the Nazi's into one of the most sadistic and cataclysmic crimes against humanity of the century, the German's genocide of the European Jewish people. Often my mother would see, or be reminded of something that would catapult her back to her time there, and she would fade away and tell me some of the things that she had experienced.

I never prompted her to talk about the details of what she had been through, maybe I should have. But why bring it up and get both of us upset talking about it.

My mom died September 11, 2004 at the age of 79. She survived the Holocaust but succumbed to cancer.

I often thought that her story needed to be told, but without knowing all the details, it would be just scratching the surface of what little we all knew.

To finally know all of her story, the things she didn't tell me, that would mean I would have to watch her video tapes, and I was never emotionally ready for that.

It's been 20 years since my mom died, and everything I now need to ask her is gone and buried next to my father in a Jewish cemetery, under a gravestone that defined their lives and is inscribed: Jorek and Rochela Blocher "Holocaust survivors."

I felt that it was about time, and my duty for me to find out what her dreadful journey was all about and share it.

Her story was something that was important and had to be told to my family, friends and the world.

It's hard to pinpoint why it was so difficult to talk about it with her. I suppose I didn't want to stir up those tragic memories of how badly she was treated and what she had endured.

It's just someplace you don't want to go, and you can just use your imagination how terrible it must have been. That's how I felt about asking my mom. I knew it was beyond horrific.

And so it took 26 years before I had the guts to watch her Shoah video. Her complete experience that was another side to her, and that most didn't know about her.

At first it was difficult for me to pick up the copy on DVD, and to put it into the player. I don't know why, but that disc weighed 1000 pounds.

I supposed that I was afraid of opening up a door that was going to potentially be really upsetting to me. I didn't want to see the factual suffering my mother had to endure, the train wreck that mangled her inner being for the rest of her life.

Why did she survive when 6 million others didn't? I think that's a question that every survivor asks themselves.

For years we (my siblings) all knew our parents were survivors and we all knew we were different from our friends. We didn't have a lot of outside family members since they were all killed. I always thought that had she been killed (or my father), neither me nor my siblings would have ever come to be. For what reason did my parents' bloodline need to continue on?

My father wrote a journal about his Holocaust experience however it was written in Yiddish and none of us could read it. It was the same situation as my mother and no one asked him to talk about it. He was quiet and never spoke about his previous family, but I often noticed him in deep thought and I wondered what secrets he was possibly keeping from us.

But my mom, she was more revealing and often spoke about things.

There were many instances where she would reflect back to her horrific time in the camps, sometimes a jab when we possibly didn't like what was for dinner, and she would remind us: "You kids would never have survived the concentration camps." That was usually enough to get us to the table.

At night when she slept, we often heard the screams from her nightmares.

Dreams that were so horrifying no one had the courage to ask her what they were about. Although, sometimes she would tell me bits of her dreams and she was always being chased by Nazis or killings in the camps.

Often, I would be riding in the car with her, and something would trigger her to talk about something that happened.

It just didn't start when I was older, and I remember being as young as 5 years old, and trapped in the car when that happened. I would just silently listen and I kept my mouth shut and my emotions inside.

Once I actually fell out of the car while she was driving my brother and I home from school. I'm not sure if I fell out on purpose or it was an accident.

I suppose it was better for her to talk about those things rather than to keep it inside as my dad did. But even though she survived, it was a dark cloud that overshadowed her life.

She really was alive and carrying on because she had to. The Germans wouldn't take everything from her and for her love for her children she carried on.

The cover photo is a photograph taken of my mother when she was 14 years old (just prior to the outbreak of the war) by her cousin Rubin Bolber, in Vilnius, Poland.

All her personal belongings were destroyed by the Nazi's including any photographs of herself and family.

Sometime after the war ended, she reconnected with her childhood friend Wanda, who had kept dear, the only remaining photograph of my mother as a child. The cover photo is that picture.

I want to mention the Nazi collaborators that helped the Nazis torture and kill Jews in Poland and all over Europe. The Lithuanian thugs, Ukrainians, Polish Police also known as the Blue police and many more, who were hired by the Nazi's to help with their extermination plans and the killing and torturing of Jews (and other prisoners) in the countries the Germans occupied. I continually refer to them and the Nazis in this book as Bastards, Sons of a bitches, Demons etc. However, in reality there is not a word that can describe the vile sewage that these entities were.

These hired lowlifes were regarded as traitors by the general public of Polish people for helping the Nazis, and I don't mean to infer that all Polish people were helping the Nazis. Many, including two Polish farmers, helped save my father's life.

Lastly, I want to speak about the sadistic Blitz Frau's of Stutthoff, a despicable group of German women who were brainwashed Nazi fanatics. Menial women, recruited to work in the concentration camps as vicious overseers of the prisoners, due to the shortage of male guards that were being pulled from concentration camp duty, and were being sent off to fight the Russians. Although most camps had their own despicable bands of Blitz Frau's, it was well documented that Stutthof (where my mom and her family was imprisoned) had one of the most heinous bunch of the most notorious, sadistic and brutally evil group of these Blitz Frau women.

They were happy to torture, abuse and execute Jews, and took their brutality towards the Jewish prisoners to an extreme level. Taking pleasure in finding new ways to torture and punish their victims.

The following are some of the evil Blitz Frau's of the Stutthof concentration camp, where my mother, aunt, grandmother and grandfather were imprisoned. There is a place in hell for these slithering bastards.

Blitz Frau Jenny Wanda Barkmann: Responsible for selecting many of the 85,000 victims, including children who would die in the gas chamber. She was also known to kill her victims with her bare hands, and beat many inmates almost to death and then sent them off to the gas chamber to die.

The other male guards couldn't even believe how cruel she was, and they nicknamed her "Mad Jenny."

She was one of the most hunted war criminals of WW2, and she was finally caught boarding a train in Gdansk, Poland, trying to escape persecution.

During her trial she flirted with her guards and vainly primped her hair and laughed as witnesses testified against her. The life of brutal violence against Jewish women and children was what gave her pleasure, and she was proficient at her job at Stutthof.

After she was captured, she was quoted to say: "Life is really a great pleasure, and pleasures don't last that long." Her lawyer called her insane, as no one in their right mind could be so sadistic, cruel and evil, even those working for the SS.

Blitz Frau Ewa Paradies: She was known to make the women prisoners undress outside in subzero conditions, and then she doused them with pails of cold water, and then forced them to stand in snow in the blistering cold for hours. If they moved she would beat them.

She personally did this to my Mother, Aunt and Grandmother. She also mercilessly brutalized inmates and took pleasure torturing Jews.

Blitz Frau Elisabeth Becker: Indoctrinated from the league of German girls. Hitler's youth "Scouts." German children who were brainwashed into becoming more loyal to Hitler's Nazi movement, rather than their parents, and they often reported their own families to the Nazi authorities for not being loyal enough to Hitler. She was also personally responsible for choosing the weakest inmates and children to die either by the gas chamber or lethal phenol injections. A sadistic, evil witch.

Blitz Frau Gerda Steinhoff: SS valued her work as a sadistic, brutal and cruel overseer of the prisoners. She selected many of the 85,000 victims to be put to death in the Stutthoff gas chamber. During her trial she repeatedly joked and laughed with her co-defendants.

Blitz Frau Wanda Klaff: Sadistically abused and tortured prisoners. Personal statement at her trial she bragged: "I am very intelligent and very devoted to my work at the camps. I struck at least two prisoners every day...." At least two, and as many more as she could take pleasure beating and torturing.

On April 25th 1946, the first war crimes tribunal was convened in Gdansk, Poland. On trial, the Blitz Frau's of Stutthof, and several other Nazi criminals for Crimes against Humanity, who served at the concentration camp Stutthof (Where my mother was imprisoned). All were found guilty and sentenced to death by hanging, which took place only a few days after their guilty verdict.

On July 4,1946, these five vile beasts, along with 6 other Nazi scum from the Stutthof concentration camp were hung to death in a public display.

The court decided, rather than a merciful long drop hanging, where the Blitz Frau's necks would snap and they would die instantly and humanely.

The execution was designed to be slow, painful and lengthy. Not a quick and easy death, but rather a sluggish, grueling strangulation, which was warranted due to the heinousness of their egregious crimes.

Eleven flatbed trucks were strategically positioned underneath each of the eleven gallows.

The criminal's legs and hands were bound with cord behind their backs, and no hoods or blind folds were used. They all sat on wooden chairs on the truck's rear bed, as the nooses were placed around their necks.

One at a time, the execution order was given for each prisoner, the truck drivers slowly drove forward until all five miscreant Biltz Frau's and the six other Nazi criminals were slowly pulled off the back of the trucks by the short ropes around their necks. Leaving them hideously jerking and spinning as they struggled to breath, and the nooses slowly tightened around their necks.

They were all agonizingly strangled on short ropes, ... and justice was served.

Chapter 1

A brisk winter storm front has quietly swept in; giant tufts of crisp fluffy white snow are steadily floating down from the sky. It is peacefully silent on the streets of Vilna tonight.

My name is Rochela Bolber. I am an adolescent teenage Jewish girl who lives an ordinary life in my extraordinary city, Vilna Poland. Most days I go to school, practice playing the piano and play hopscotch on the sidewalk with my little sister, Jenya.

Other than listening to the radio, there isn't much else to do, but fortunately I love to read books and go with my friends to see movies at the local movie house. I especially love books and movies that take me far away from my ordinary life, so I can see and read about other fantastic places in the world, such as America. I wish I could visit there someday, and go to Hollywood!

I live with my Mamma Gitel and Pappa Yeruchim along with my two sisters Cyla and Jenya, in a three room apartment located at 3548 Yagellowska Street. Jenya, my adorable little sister, is only six, and Cyla, my older sister who antagonizes me to no end is sixteen. Two years older than me.

My Pappa jokes that he is completely surrounded by women, but I never heard him complain once that he would have wanted a son. He was happy that he had three daughters to love.

I just left Steinberg's Candy Shop, where I had spent all of my Hanukkah gelt on a big bag full of hard candy, gumdrops and a bundle of string licorice for my little sister, Jenya. My little sister Jenya is my special little darling. I love her so much, and we are very close. I've been taking care of her since she was born, since my Mamma had a lot to do, taking care of the apartment and all of us. When Jenya is sick or falls down and gets hurt, she calls for me, not my Mamma.

I always thought of her as my "little baby" sister and I promised her that I will always be there for her, forever. However, my older sister Cyla, is a different story, we are not close at all. She tends to be a trouble maker and always looking out for herself. She is shifty and sly, and boy can she spin the yarn! You might say she was gifted at the art of making up a story, some might call her a polished liar, and as the saying goes….She could easily sell ice to an Eskimo!

As the snow continues to fall, it is a mystery to me.

How does a frozen raindrop transform itself into such a complicated work of art? It puzzled me when our teacher told us that no two snowflakes are exactly alike. How does anyone really know that for sure? It's not as if we can examine every snowflake that has ever fallen from the sky to prove it. As far as I'm concerned, a snowflake is a snowflake, and they all look the same to me.

For now, my only hopes and dreams are growing up in a kind hearted world, reading magical books, becoming a famous piano player, marrying a prince, watching movies at the cinema with my friends and being with my little sister, Jenya forever, because I love her so much. And possibly finding two snowflakes that are exactly alike!

Suddenly, I hear snow crunching and footsteps quickening behind me as I walk. A flash of fear rises into my chest and my heart begins pounding, which only subsides once I recognise that uncontrollable giggle. It is my best friend, Wanda. Suddenly, I feel ice cold mittens cover my eyes from behind.

"I am the Dybbuk of Vilna, the evil ghost spirit and collector of Jewish teenage souls! Give me some candy or I will haunt you forever!" she giggled in a spooky voice.

"Are you crazy, you could have given me a heart attack, Wanda! Besides, I already live with the Dybbuk, her name is Cyla!" I joked. My older sister, Cyla, loves to antagonize me.

"I know you heard me coming, Rochelka! Give me a gum drop, or I'll throw a snowball in your face!" she jokingly demanded. I reached into my bag and gave her a handful of candy. Then she grabbed hold of my arm and vigorously tugged me along behind her, up the dimly lit street towards our apartment building. As we were running, I was watching the snowflakes fall through the light beams of the tall street lights.

"Come on, hurry, and stop staring up into the sky, Rochelka! We have to get home and decorate my Christmas tree!" she exclaimed.

Tomorrow night is Christmas eve, and like every year before, I am invited to help decorate Wanda's Christmas tree. It has become a friendship tradition of ours. However, it's odd for me to hang crucifixes and statuary images of Jesus and Mary on the limbs of a Christmas tree. It's different from what I'm used to, mainly celebrating Hanukkah and Jewish holidays.

Her mother also serves lots of fancy cakes and pastries from the restaurant that they own. I'll sneak some home for Jenya and my Pappa!

Wanda and I have been friends since we were little girls. We are both 14, and could pass for sisters. Well, except for the fact that I have black hair and Wanda is blonde. It doesn't matter that we practice different religions, me being Jewish and her being Catholic. We have perfect chemistry and we grew up together in the same apartment building. We both play the piano, and we both love to read books and go to the movies together on the weekends, preferably Saturday nights after Sabbath for me.

Despite not attending the same school – Wanda going to Catholic school and me going to public school with mostly Jewish kids– she has always been my best friend. But most of all we have each other's backs.

A horse drawn sleigh with jingling bells trots by as I try to stop and catch a few more snowflakes on my tongue. It's my favorite time of the year – everything is so quiet and peaceful. I love the feeling of being bundled up on a frigid night, while the heavy snowflakes silently fall from heaven, and I'm walking on the soft snow covered sidewalks under the diffused moonlight. Most everyone was home preparing for the holidays. This year, 1938, the day before Christmas Eve and the Sabbath just so happened to fall on the same day.

"Come on Rochel! My grandfather will be angry if we are late! He already hates the Jews because he says your people are taking over the city!" Wanda joked.

"Yes, actually my father who is a roofer is stealing the roofs off the Polish citizens' homes so he can re-sell them new ones!" I laughed.

Our community is heavily populated with Jews. My neighborhood and school are peaceful, and a happy place to live. I never experienced much antisemitism, except from Wanda's grandfather. We aren't "rich Jews," as some of the Polish townspeople maliciously referred to us as, but we aren't poor either. My Pappa, who is a roofer, has some money saved to buy us a house someday. He makes sure Cyla always has fine new coats, clothes, and shoes. It's practical for me and Jenya to get hand-me-downs but he often surprises us with new things from the big department store across the street from us. There are all sorts of restaurants and a variety of stores in my neighborhood.

My Mamma would shop at Shapiro's for meat and there was an open air market, where she would buy bread, fruits and vegetables.

My friend Wanda's parents own a restaurant down the street where we would sometimes stop for some sort of tasty treat. My neighborhood was a peaceful and happy place to live, and I love it here!

There is one very rich Jewish person in our building though, his name is Mr. Sugarman. He owns the building, and lives in a very large apartment on the top floor. He outfits his family with very expensive clothes, and his wife is adorned with lavish Jewelry. He has 2 maids, and a chef to cook their food! There is even a nanny for his 3 children, and their toys are the envy of the town. Now Mr. Sugarman, he was a rich Jew! With all his money though, there is just one thing missing from his life, happiness. His wife is cold as ice and I never see him playing with his children. He assumes that he was paying a nanny to do that for him, I suppose.

Wanda and I arrived at our building and we temporarily parted ways on the staircase.

"I have to help my mother set the table and light the Sabbath candles. I'll eat quickly, and I promise I'll come right over!" I shouted.

I burst into our apartment and heard my little sister practicing her piano lesson and my mother and older sister setting the table.

"Hurry Rochelka, the food is getting cold! Where have you been? It's almost Sabbath!" my Mamma scolded.

My sister Cyla was smirking, as if she had something poisonous to say:

"So, my friend Helen Steinberg, you know, whose father owns the candy shop, told me you were in their store earlier, and you wasted ALL your Hanukkah gelt on candy! That was very irresponsible of you, and you're going to rot out your teeth, brat! Pappa's not going to like it when he hears that you wasted all your money on foolish candy! You will surely get the strap for that!" she snickered.

"It's utterly amazing how gossip travels so fast in my neighborhood!!" I thought to myself.

Suddenly, I panicked, I had to get rid of the candy! So I ran into my room and threw all the candy out the window (except the liquorice), to get rid of the incriminating evidence. Then I calmly returned with the paper bag:

"Cyla, my sister, you're such a liar! All that I bought was some licorice for Jenya!"

Cyla grabbed the brown bag and was miffed that all that was in there was a few strands of licorice.

"Here Jenya, this is for my 'favorite' sister," I grinned.

Pappa came barging into the apartment and shook the snow off his coat and handed it to me to hang in the closet. I loved his coat, especially the mink fur collar that wrapped around it. Sometimes when I'm cold at night I wrap it around me like a blanket and nuzzle with the mink collar! I love my life and my family so much, even my sister Cyla, but my Pappa, he especially meant the world to me. He showered me with so much love, it often made my older sister jealous. I think he loved all of us the same, but I really loved my Papa more than life itself, and I believe he knows that.

There was one morning when my Pappa was walking me to school, and our Rabbi crossed our path.

"Yeruchim, I didn't see you at morning service this morning, and now it's going to cost you. I'm going to make you an offer to even your score with God for being a bad Jew. I want to buy your precious little girl, Rochel, to be my daughter. I have lots of money in my pocket! How much will you sell her to me for?" he joked.

"Well it's up to her if she wants to leave me. I suppose the synagogue could use a beautiful angel like my Rochel floating around the ark. Ask her how much she wants," he jokingly replied.

Both men smiled and stared at me for my response.

"Rabbi, I will not leave my Pappa for even 1 million paper Zlotes! In fact, not even for one million Zlotes in COINS!" I firmly stated.

Both men laughed at my child minded reply, especially that I thought 1 million coins was worth more than 1 million in paper money.

My Pappa is the type of father that holds us often, tells us how much he loves us and jokes with us all the time.

He often tells us stories from when he was a young boy. Usually there is a lesson or a moral to his stories, but sometimes they are just funny. He loves my Mamma very much, and they have a wonderful marriage.

After all, my Mamma is a very beautiful woman. Oddly, she was once married to my Pappa's brother, who died early into their marriage, possibly from an illness. The marriage law back then was: "If you were single and your married brother died, you were obligated to marry your sister in law," and that's how they were married. I often thought that if my Mamma's first husband had not passed away, neither me nor my sisters would exist.

"Let's eat, I'm starving, Gittel!" he shouted.

My Mamma lit the Sabbath candles while I quickly set up his plate at the head of the table, and we each sat down at our places.

My place was next to my Pappa and Jenya sat next to me. My sister Cyla would sit on the opposite side of Pappa, struggling to get some attention from him with her phony patronizing conversation.

"I think you'll be so proud of me, Pappa! Today, I outsmarted my teacher. I had told her that Rochelka had taken my homework to school, and she turned it into her teacher by mistake, and I have to wait till Monday to get it back from her to hand in! She believed me, and gave me an extension on my essay!" Cyla gloated.

My father sternly gazed at her:

"That's supposed to make me proud of you? That you are a liar!" my father scolded and shook his head in disbelief.

I pretended to be disappointed as well, as I held back my laughter as my sister got yelled at.

Mamma placed our meal on the table, and I took a few spoonfuls of meat and potatoes on my plate before quickly eating it all up. Suddenly, there was a frantic knock at the door. I rushed over to answer it, and it was Wanda, anxiously standing there. She was bouncing up and down as if she was going to pee herself!

"Hurry up, let's go! It's time to decorate the Christmas tree!!"

"Mamma, I'm going to Wanda's!" I shouted, as I ran out the door!

Together, hand in hand we raced up the stairs to Wanda's apartment, and burst through the door and into her apartment. Instantly I smelled the sweet evergreen aroma that filled the room. Her Grandfather was sitting in his chair smoking a pipe, and sneered when he saw me enter. Wanda's mother and father were quite nice though, and always made me feel welcome.

"Shalom Shabbat, Rochelka," her father jokingly chuckled.

I smiled and didn't bother to correct him that it was said in reverse and supposed to be "Shabbat Shalom," as it would have been disrespectful. "Merry Christmas, Mr. & Mrs. Rodge!" I replied.

In the corner of the room stands a freshly cut evergreen tree, mounted in a tree stand with paper boxes of last year's tree ornaments wrapped in tissue paper set beside it.

"I want to go first!" shouted Wanda.

"Rochelka is our guest, Wanda. She should go first, then you can have a turn," stated her mother.

"First one ornament, then the Jew girl will take over the whole Christmas tree!" her grandfather gripped.

I awkwardly smiled as Wanda passed the box of Christmas ornaments to me. I closed my eyes and reached into the box and took hold of a wrapped item. "Please God, don't let it be Jesus or Mary," I prayed.

When I opened the tissue paper, I was relieved to see that it was a ceramic tile that said, "Merry Christmas from Vilna," and I carefully hung it on a branch of the tree. The box was passed between myself, Wanda and her parents. I felt as if we were playing a game of Russian Roulette: each time I picked a wrapped ornament, I was relieved that it was not a crucifix or a religious figure.

I had some idea in my head that if I hung a Christian ornament, Swiety Mikolaj "Saint Nicholas" would come down our chimney and drop off Christmas gifts at our apartment, and I would have a lot of explaining to do to my Pappa if that ever happened!

When we finished decorating, Wanda's mother brought out some grape juice with raisin cookies and pastries on a crystal tray.

She had already made a little bag of goodies for my little sister, since she knew I was going to ask.

Finally they sang Christmas carols and Wanda taught me Cicha noc "Silent night" which I sang, but felt awkward and mumbled through some of the parts.

Afterwards, while we sat in her room and played with dolls, we talked about the cute boys who lived on our block, especially Issac Golstein.

He is 4 years older than us, and so handsome, but he is my sister Cyla's crush and off limits. Suddenly, there was a rapid knock at their front door. It was Cyla.

"Time for Rochelka to come home, my father wants to punish her for cheating on her bible studies exam," she announced boldly so that everyone would hear.

I gathered my things, and as I approached my sister at the doorway, I turned to Wanda's parents and I thanked them for inviting me.

"By the way my falshe' (phony) sister, you are a big fat liar, I haven't had a bible exam in weeks!" Cyla shrugged her shoulders. "Must have been your math exam, darling," she countered.

Sometimes I really can't stand my big sister. Actually, most times!

"Merry Christmas, everyone," I shouted as we left.

"Merry Christmas....to us!" rudely replied her grandfather, as we left the apartment.

Chapter 2

Spring 1939. Joyfully, we are preparing for my favorite holiday, Passover. It's a difficult transition, since we have to clean the countertops and cabinets to get rid of all the bread and pastry items. In Yiddish we call it "Chametz." Technically all items made with yeast and flour are supposed to be sold off to gentiles (non-Jews), but my Pappa just gives it to the men who work for him. The rules surrounding this holiday are so strict that we actually have to replace our dishes and flatware with a separate set that are exclusive for Passover use only. I always wondered and asked my Mamma what would happen if I accidentally used the wrong tea cup.

She joked, "One of Moses's 10 plagues will come to get you!"

My Mamma is very superstitious about religious rituals: everything has to be by the book or else something terrible is going to happen. She is always terrified during Rosh Hashanah and Yom Kippur that God might not give us a good year if we don't fast and go to synagogue. My favorite part of this holiday is the special Passover food and goodies my Mamma makes. She is a fantastic cook and always prepares my favorite meals and Passover desserts. Kreplach, plums with peanuts, and my personal favorite, sponge cake, is always our family tradition.

The day before Passover was about to begin, my Mamma asked me to bring two bottles of wine to my uncle Gidalias' bakery for his seder.

My mother entrusting me with such an important item made me feel important and grown-up. As I left the apartment, I heard my mother shout out:

"Cyla, go with Rochelka!" And my bubble burst.

With my older sister tagging along, it would appear that I needed someone to hold my hand.

Nevertheless, I hid the two bottles under my coat, and pressed them against my chest with my arms crossed to conceal the bottles from public view. I didn't want to take any chances that some drunken bully would take them from me, so it was better to keep them hidden. We were almost at my uncle's bakery when my sister noticed a policeman standing at the street corner, right in front of my uncle's bakery shop.

With a dramatic tone that only my sister could muster up, she opened her mouth and initiated her devious plan to take the wine from me.

"Look Rochelka, a policeman is right in front of the bakery! He is going to be suspicious of why you are walking with your hands across your coat, and when he finds out that you are carrying wine, and at your age, he will arrest you and throw you in jail for sure!" she harshly stated.

"Oh no! What should I do?" I sarcastically begged her.

"Give me the bottles since I am older. The policeman will not bother me for having wine, and I will give it back to you before we go into the bakery," she deviously stated.

I knew immediately what she was up to. She was steaming that Mamma entrusted me with the wine, and she wanted to be the "Big shot giver" to our uncle.

The closer we walked toward the young police officer, the more persistent Cyla became and demanded that I hand over the wine to her. Finally, we were past the point of no return and I was standing right in front of the officer. I decided to be clever and appear to the policeman as if I wasn't holding anything under my coat, so I reached out one arm to shake hands with him.

"Good afternoon officer, I hope you are having a fine day," I cheerfully stated.

Suddenly, both bottles of wine slipped down through my coat and shattered on the ground at the policeman's feet! My sister and I both cringed as wine splattered all over our shoes and stockings, including all over the police officers' shoes and pants! I froze, waiting to get dragged off to the police station. Suddenly, Uncle Gidalia intervened with a box of pastries he quickly snatched from the counter of his bakery, and presented it to the officer.

"I'm so sorry officer, my niece has butter fingers, but I have a box of delicious treats for you and your family." The young officer seemed to let go of the issue and he thanked my uncle. Uncle Gidalia pulled me into his shop while my sister remained outside with the police officer. Schmoozing and flattering him, to sway him not to arrest me, or possibly to get a date out of it.

"Are you okay?" my uncle nervously questioned.

The whole ordeal was so overwhelming to me, and now as I feared going to jail, I also realized that I failed my mission to deliver the wine to my uncle. I began to cry.

"Don't be upset, Rochelka. I don't know why, but I suppose your sister Cyla may have had something to do with this. Don't worry, I have plenty of wine for Passover. Here, take some Passover treats back with you and enjoy your holiday," my uncle kindly stated.

I was so grateful, I hugged him so tightly and I ran off past my sister who was still chatting and carrying on with the policeman. I went straight home. My mother was happy to see that I returned with a box of Passover treats, and I mentioned nothing about the wine. Oddly when Cyla returned she said nothing as well.

She obviously didn't want anyone to know she was fraternizing with a Polish police officer, and was possibly meeting up with him for a date.

Chapter 3

September 1939. My classmates and I were all in our classroom quietly reading books. I was sitting next to my girlfriend Rivka, when our teacher Mr. Pachinko was called outside by another teacher, Mr. Sklade, who had a stern look of concern. They were both Jews and spoke quietly together in Yiddish. They chatted for a few moments then both teachers reentered the classroom. Mr. Pachinko spoke:

"Attention children, this morning the Germans invaded the eastern portion of Poland, while the Russians invaded the western side where we are situated. The government is calling for adult volunteers to help with the fight to protect Poland from these barbarians."

Some of the Polish boys became upset and asked permission to leave, while most of us just sat there worried and confused. To quiet things down Mr. Pachinko kept us at school till the end of the day or until our parents arrived to take us home.

Incredibly, it only took 3 days for Poland to succumb to the invasion and the war was over. I never heard a gunshot or a bomb go off. Germany easily took over eastern Poland, and Russia took control of the western half.

We were relieved that the Russians were here rather than the Germans after hearing about the atrocities they had been committing against the

Jewish people in other European countries under their control. We were well aware of Kristallnacht and the antisemitism pouring out of Germany. The way we got our information was mostly by word of mouth and sometimes newspapers. One thing was for certain: we were better off than the Jews on the Eastern side of Poland.

The Russians were with us for 2 years. Under the Russian occupation things didn't change much for us, and we were happy considering the alternative.

For the most part, the Russian soldiers were very kind to us and some actually moved their families from Russia to be with them. It was funny to see the Russian women buy nightgowns from the department stores and wear them out on the streets, thinking that they were formal dresses. I suppose under Stalin, they weren't used to the luxuries we had here in Poland. The Russian men were joyful people, despite the hard conditions in Russia, and it wasn't uncommon for a group of soldiers to begin singing Russian songs and to begin dancing in groups on the streets of our city. One of my friends once asked a Russian soldier if they had "coffee" in Russia. The soldier lit up and boasted with pride, and stated:

"Not only do we have coffee in Russia, but we also have matches!"

When I heard that he was gloating about having a pack of matches, it didn't seem that they had a very good life in their communist country.

As time went on though, food was becoming more and more scarce, and it was more challenging to eat as well as we once did.

We were given food ration cards and had to wait in long lines to receive bread or whatever else was available that day, which often ran out. At least my family was safe and together. My friends and I were still able to get together at the cinema, which was sometimes open.

One evening, near the end of the Russian occupation, I was practicing my piano when there was a soft knock at the door.

My sister Cyla shouted to me from our bedroom to see who was knocking at the door. I begrudgingly got up from my piano and opened the door. My jaw dropped. It was Issac Golstein!

He was standing there with a bouquet of flowers and a small box of candy! I didn't know what to say, and to my dire disappointment, I knew he must have come to call on my sister Cyla.

"Hello Issac, I'll go tell Cyla you are here," I sadly stated. But before I could run off, he grabbed my hand!

"It's not Cyla, I'm here to call on. Beautiful Rochelka, I've had a crush on you since you were a young girl and now that you are older, I've come here to ask for your father's permission to court you. Would you allow me to escort you to the summer concert this weekend?" he quietly stated.

I was overcome by a rush of joy and happiness, a feeling that I had never experienced before. There was a handsome boy at my door who thought I was beautiful, and wanted to court me!

I was lost for words in a wonderful way, when suddenly I heard my sister charge out of her room. She had heard everything and was determined to ruin it for me. She was storming down the hallway, and she abruptly stopped at the entrance into our living room. She was stunned to see Issac Golstein standing at our doorway, holding my hand and flirting with me as he held a bouquet of flowers and candy. Her jealousy began to boil.

"Rochelka, you are such a little snot, when a guest comes to visit ME, you should not just stand there scratching your butt and wasting his time blabbing with a little turd such as yourself," she wickedly stated.

I was so embarrassed! My face instantly turned beet red, and I let go of his hand and ran away, locking myself in my closet.

I heard the front door slam and heavy footsteps going down the stairs and my sister chasing after him. "Issac! I'm the one for you, not my snotty little half-wit sister!" she called out.

Deeply disappointed, he kept walking down the stairs and he threw the flowers and candy down on the steps.

I heard the main entrance door open then slam closed, and then the heavy steps of my sister returning to our apartment. My Mamma came out to see what all the commotion was all about.

Cyla returned carrying the disheveled bouquet and the broken box of chocolates that Issac had thrown down the stairs.

"Look Mamma! Issac Golstein came to visit and left me these beautiful flowers and chocolates! I think he came to court me, but Rochelka insulted him and chased him away!" she falsely stated.

I couldn't look at her, let alone speak to her for some time. She was such a selfish person. It's no wonder Issac wanted me over her.

Chapter 4

The Russian occupation lasted for 2 years. We had heard horrible stories about the Germans and the killing of innocent Jews, but no one could believe that such evil could actually exist. We hoped that the horrendous stories were exaggerated. Occasionally there were practice drills and air raid sirens that would go off, and we were supposed to hide in the basements of our houses. No one ever thought that the Germans' would be foolish enough to attack the Russians, so we didn't take the sirens seriously.

It was exactly one week since Issac came to call on me.

I'll never forget the date: June 22,1941, when the sirens went off. I wasn't concerned though, because these drills sounded off often, and nothing ever happened.

However, this day was different. Suddenly, as I was walking across the street from my apartment building, I heard a loud whistling noise coming from the sky, and then a huge explosion came from the area behind our building. It was followed by hundreds more of the whistling bombs hitting random sites all around our city. It created chaos as thousands of panic-stricken people were desperately running aimlessly in all directions, searching for places to hide from the exploding bomb shells. There were barrages of loud explosions, smoke, and fires breaking out everywhere. I ran alone throughout the street, searching for a place to hide as bombs exploded all around me. Through the smoke, I saw masses of contorted, bloody, dead bodies scattered everywhere. Some of the victims were crawling with no legs bleeding to death and pleading for help.

Then tragically, I saw Issac Golstein, lying lifeless next to his twisted bicycle, under a portion of a building's brick wall that had exploded and landed on top of him, crushing him to death.

I ran into a tiny stone storage shed next to our building, where wood and coal was kept. I knelt inside, clinging to the stone wall as I held my hands over my ears to cover up the sounds of the loud explosions and people screaming.

"Why is God allowing this to happen?" I cried to myself. I feared the worst, that we were all going to die. Then I noticed a young woman who lived in my building, scrambling in front of us and carrying a small child. She ran past me, and I called to her to hide with me.

Then I saw that she had no idea that her child had been hit by a piece of shrapnel, and the child's arm was dangling like a raw piece of bloody meat, and her blood was pouring everywhere. Another bomb exploded and they were both gone.

I placed my hands on my head and clenched my hair. "Is this the beginning of our end, for us?" I shouted to God. But there was no answer.

Chapter 5

The following day, big German tanks rolled into our city. The Russian soldiers ran off with their families back to Russia. Along with them went Poles and Jews who were mobile enough to travel alone. My father considered leaving Vilna, but with a wife and 3 daughters he felt it would be a greater challenge not knowing anyone or having any family to help us once we got there. From what he heard, life wasn't so great in Russia, either. My cousin Rubin, who was a photographer, was one of the lucky ones that got away. And later migrated to France where he met a beautiful French woman, Germaine, who he later married.

How bad could it be with the Germans? Maybe a lot of what we heard really was exaggerated. After all, killing innocent unarmed men women and children didn't seem believable or conceivable. So like thousands of other families, we stayed.

When the tanks stopped, a miserable German SS commandant got out of his staff car plastered with Nazi swastikas all over it. He ordered that all the Jews were to wear yellow Star of David patches on our sleeves, and to stay off the sidewalks. We could only walk in the street gutter. If caught without the star badge or walking on the sidewalk, we would face fatal consequences. Just then, he pulled out his pistol and pointed his gun at an old Jewish store keeper who was standing on the sidewalk in front of his shop. The

Nazi pulled the trigger, and shot the man in the belly! The old man clenched his stomach, buckled over and fell to the ground. Everyone screamed and scattered off the sidewalk and into the street gutter. Now we were considered lesser than animals, only allowed to walk in the street gutter where the horses and cattle traveled.

The gutter area was littered with animal excrement, trash and mud. In his view, it was the only place fit for a Jew to walk.

The non-Jewish Polish people had nothing to worry about, and had no fear of German persecution. Some were happy to lend a hand and help round up the Jews. In fact, the Germans didn't actually know who were Jews in our city, and left it to the Polish police to help identify us.

The Germans required slave labor and immediately began grabbing men for work details, mostly digging. If you resisted you were shot dead in the street, but most wanted to work since they believed it would save them. The Nazis and Polish police were now indiscriminately arresting older or defiant men, and carting them off to jail and then to Ponary. Ponary was a wooded area outside of town that was often used as a nature retreat for rest and relaxation. Now it has been turned into a killing zone for unfortunate Jews.

One late afternoon, I decided to take a walk to my friend Rivka's house, which was only a few blocks away. It was raining and the horse path was flooded with mud and animal excrement, so I took a chance and stayed on the sidewalk. Suddenly I felt a large hand grab onto my shoulder. It was Wanda's grandfather.

"Get off the sidewalk, Jew girl! Your kind belongs in the gutter!" he scowled and he shoved me down into the mud, and I fell on top of a pile of wet horse manure. I stood up trying to keep my composure as a few people walked by and laughed. I stuck my tongue out at him and hopped back on the sidewalk and ran as fast as I could to Rivka's house.

When her mother opened the door, she was shocked and angry that I risked my life to come over and visit Rivka, especially since it was past curfew. But I was young and naive and maybe a little courageous.

"You could have been arrested and taken to Ponary, foolish girl! Not only that, but you could have gotten all of us arrested and killed! Why are you covered in mud and you smell like cow manure?" she exclaimed.

"It's a long story…but it's horse manure," I sadly replied. I turned around, and made my way back home. I made sure to take the side streets and not to be seen.

When I got home my mamma was waiting for me with the strap, and that night I learned a valuable lesson not to take dangerous risks. The times have changed, the Russians are gone, and now we are under the rule of demons. One wrong turn to the left or right could cost the life of yourself and your family.

The following morning, there was loud knocking coming from down the hallway of our apartment building. I could hear people shouting and begging. The knocking would pause, then continue to the next apartment and so on. As it traveled down the hallway, the same tumult from each apartment continued.

Finally, there was a loud knock at our door and my father reluctantly opened the door. Stanislaw, the Polish building superintendent was sadly standing there with a Polish police officer. He was holding papers with German script plastered all over it.

"What's going on, Stan?" my father fearfully inquired.

"I'm so sorry, Yeruchim. The Germans are ordering all the Jews to leave their homes at once. Pack what you can carry. They are moving you all to the ghetto they established across town," he somberly stated.

"What ghetto across town? Across town is where all the poor people live!" exclaimed my Pappa.

"I'm sorry to say that they were all evicted to make room for the rest of the Vilna Jews, and now they may be vacationing in Ponary. Their homes are empty and the area is all fenced in with barbed wire. You have an hour to be on the streets with your belongings," he firmly stated.

My mother began to shriek and fainted into my father's arms, causing my little sister to cry. Cyla ran to look out the window, and I followed her. The scene was horrifying. All of our Jewish neighbors were being physically thrown out of their apartments and homes and cast out into the streets. There was nothing we could do but quickly pack the things we could carry in suitcases. My mother put together as much food as she could pack in a sack. The last item I took was my toothbrush, which I placed in the pocket of my skirt. With the Germans dehumanizing us, I felt that my toothbrush was my item of humanity. When we left our apartment, I saw Wanda crying at the end of the hallway as her grandfather held her back from running to me.

"Don't worry my friend, next Christmas I'll be back and we'll decorate your tree again!" I shouted to her as we were brutally shuffled out of the building by Polish policemen.

The streets were in chaos as the Jewish families struggled with their bundles of belongings. It was difficult for the elderly and parents with small children to navigate along, while desperately clinging to all that they had left in this world.

There were Nazi box trucks that were traveling up and down the roadside with a loud speaker: "Attention Juden (Jews), there is no need for you to struggle with your belongings! We are happy to assist you. Write your names on your belongings and they will be safely transported, and delivered to your new home in the ghetto.

You will be able to reclaim your personal items and belongings!" the crass voice blared from the loud speakers.

Everyone did what they were told, and allowed the Germans and their henchmen to scribble the families names on their bundles, and then they were tossed into the back of awaiting trucks.

Most were apprehensive since their Jewelry, money and everything they owned were in those bundles. But there was no real choice in the matter.

Brigades of Nazi SS with attack dogs began sweeping through the buildings searching for hiding families that were refusing to leave. I saw my school teacher Mr. Pichinko and his wife were being dragged out of their building as she clutched her baby. They, and dozens of others were viciously rounded up and thrown into the street.

The men were then lined up against the wall of the old synagogue by Nazi gunmen, and immediately executed with machine guns! His wife was begging for her baby's life, as they too were brutally shoved along with other women and children towards the wall, tripping over their husbands' and fathers' dead bodies.

A Nazi official approached her and smiled as if was going to show her some compassion, and he tried to confiscate her baby. She held her baby tightly and refused to let her go. He then shouted something in German to the dog handlers, and two dogs were released and attacked the woman and the baby, ripping them to shreds as if they were disposable dog toys.

Everyone stood there just watching in horror and disbelief. What could anyone do? They had guns and vicious dogs. We had prayers and God.

That Nazi scum chuckled as he enjoyed the mauling as some sort of sick sport, and then with the wave of his hand he ordered the remainder of the hiding women and children machine gunned down. We were horrified. We now understood that unlike the Russian occupiers, the Germans were evil bloodthirsty bastards. It was afternoon when they gave the order for us to move out and they herded us through the streets of Vilna as if we were cattle going to slaughter.

The Polish townspeople lined the streets, watching and waiting for us to leave. Some were sad and horrified, but others took pleasure charging into our vacated apartments and pilfering whatever they could carry out. Some even fought each other for some of the prized possessions such as an ice box or mattresses.

We watched tragically as we saw our furniture, clothes and personal belongings being looted by our neighbors. We all thought this was a bad dream and couldn't possibly be happening.

It took a day and a half of walking to reach the ghetto, and we all slept on the ground in a park that night. I thought about how smart I was to take my toothbrush, so I could brush my teeth the following morning.

There were hundreds if not thousands of us all together, but there was one common question everyone was asking…what was going to become of us?

Chapter 6

We began to enter a gray dead zone in our once beautiful city. What was once a bustling community, populated with religious Jews and Jewish merchants, was now reduced to a Nazi military compound with desolate streets, empty shot-up buildings, and pools of blood everywhere.

We saw the large barbed wire gates in the distance. On one hand, we were relieved to rest and stop walking, but it was overshadowed by the fear of our survival. The gates were open and heavily guarded by Nazi SS with German Shepherd dogs, barking and snapping at us. There were so many people, you couldn't walk without bumping into someone. Everyone was confused and fearful for their families future.

I saw Mr. Sugarman, the wealthy owner of our building, and his lavishly dressed wife and children moving along through the crowd. I thought how ironic, that the richest man in the building with all his money was now reduced to a Jew peasant like us. All his money couldn't get him out of this mess.

They immediately forced us into lines, and asked me questions about my Pappa. Apparently, being a roofer made him an important Jew and he was given working papers which would be invaluable for us. They let us go into the ghetto, but there was another line that was sending people to work camps.

Men were rushing to get on to the trucks, which they believed would take them to work. They believed, if they could work, they would be taken care of and working would spare them from being killed.

On the contrary, those trucks ultimately took all the people to Ponary, to be executed in the woods.

Someone had left a message scratched into the paint of the truck which read, "They are killing us!" None of the volunteers ever returned.

My father miraculously found a place for us to stay: a 5-room apartment which had been vacated. Chairs were knocked over and I noticed that the clock on the wall spring was unwound and stopped at 2:13. The rest of the rooms were pillaged and the furniture was all gone. The rooms were all inhabited by other displaced families. We were lucky to find a place, but the availability was low and extremely overcrowded. Besides the kitchen, each room had 4 corners. In each corner, a family resided. Twenty families (approximately 80 people) were occupying this 5 room apartment, including my family. We tried to work together considering we were all in the same boat. However, there was constant quarreling in the kitchen: try to imagine 20 families preparing their dinner ration all at the same time.

The German's strategy was to turn us against each other.

The rules of the ghetto were strict. If you were noticed outside after the curfew, you would likely be either beaten to near death or sent for a ride to Ponary.

The ghetto had a government and was run by a group of profound Jews that were put in place by the Polish police. It was called the JudenRat. They appointed a person to hand out ration cards, so there was something, although minimal, for us to eat. After all, we couldn't work if we had no food.

I remember receiving a ration of strange dark red meat which we assumed to be horse meat. It was so dark and ugly but we ate it. We went from being a strictly kosher household to scavengers who would eat almost anything now.

Due to my father's designation as "an important Jew," he was allowed to leave the ghetto to work as a carpenter. He had a non-Jewish acquaintance who happened to be responsible for handing out the German documents which permitted these exits. The document was difficult to come by, and it needed to have an Ausweiger stamp (working permit), stamped on the paper. We actually had two sets of those papers, although it was strictly one per family. My father's friend slipped him an extra one for my Uncle Gadalia, since he was alone and not part of a family group. He could possibly have been sent to Ponary. To solve this problem, Uncle Gadalia came up with the idea to say that Cyla was his wife, despite there being a very broad age difference between the two. No one expected the Germans would check the details of each Ausweiger document, as people came and went. However, the Germans paid strict attention to details of everything, including work papers to come and go.

My father, Uncle Gadalia, Cyla and I were working by day, and moving in and out of the ghetto freely. I was working in the sewing house with Cyla and my father was doing carpentry. Fortunately, we all returned each night and were happy to see each other alive. We never knew what to expect with the Germans and who they might kill.

It was difficult in the apartment at night when everyone came home from working. Twenty families were trying to use the kitchen to make what little food they had for their families, and there began to be fights amongst themselves.

Sometimes while we were out of the ghetto, there were opportunities to trade with the local citizens for some food. Some tried to sneak it back into the ghetto.

However, if the Nazi collaborating Lithuanian guards found that you were trying to smuggle food back into the ghetto, they would immediately confiscate it and you would get something they called "25." That was 25 cracks with a bull whip or a club.

Those animals made you count aloud each blow they dealt out, however usually no one made it past number 3, but they would continue to be beaten even though they were unconscious.

My girlfriend, Sonia, was caught coming in with a slice of bread in her binder. The Lithuanian guards had just returned from murdering an entire small village of Jews in a nearby town. They were tired and had had enough blood for the day and miraculously let her go.

Uncle Gildalia wasn't so lucky when he tried to smuggle an apple in, he got his "25" and couldn't sit for two weeks.

Things were becoming routine in the ghetto, but you could never relax. We would all leave the ghetto together (myself, Cyla my Father, and Uncle Gadalia) until one dreadful morning there was a vicious Nazi waiting at the gate, randomly inspecting the Ausweiger documents. When my sister Cyla went through with my Uncle, the Nazi shouted, "Halt!" and stopped them with his boney finger and analyzed the document with his flimsy wire rimmed glasses.

My father broke down, as he saw the handwriting on the wall and began wailing, "I lost my daughter, Cyla! They are going to kill her!" he cried uncontrollably and repeated it over and over!

The Nazi grabbed Cyla's hair, and looked Cyla over and then my Uncle.

"Are you trying to tell me this old man is your husband? You are liars! This man looks old enough to be your grandfather!" he shouted.

He then turned and motioned to his henchmen, and they raised their guns and aimed them at my sister and uncle.

My father collapsed as he couldn't bear to watch Cyla get executed. The Nazi nodded at a soldier and pointed at my uncle. They immediately dragged him away and took him to "the kill room," which was a meat locker in a vacant butcher shop, where they held people to be executed.

Miraculously, they both survived. They freely let my sister go, but my uncle immediately saw an opportunity and he escaped. As they were entering the butcher shop, other soldiers were dragging in another Jew behind my uncle who was fighting as hard as he could. The Nazi vermin let go of Gadalia, to help with the resisting Jew, and my uncle managed to slip out of the building and he escaped.

He was still imprisoned in the ghetto though, and weeks later they caught up with him hiding in the basement of an old hardware store. They dragged him out and shot him dead in the street for everyone to see.

When the sacred Jewish holiday Yom Kippur arrived, we tried to have a makeshift religious service.

There were plenty of Rabbis available, but it was maliciously organized by the Nazi's to be the first day of the ghettos' sadistic extermination of Jews. Conveniently chosen to take place on our holiest day. They came in with trucks and violently abducted hundreds of Jews and took them to Ponary to kill. This continued every time there was a Jewish holiday. They called it a "clean out."

A short time later, the Nazi's formed what they called, "the little ghetto."

My sister and I returned from working at the sewing house one evening, and we were told that the big ghetto was closed.

We were directed to the little ghetto to spend the night. It was formed a few blocks away to temporarily separate the working Jews from the rest of the population in the big ghetto.

When we arrived at the little ghetto, we immediately searched for my father.

We were so happy when he called out to us. We saw an open doorway in a vacant apartment building; it was deathly silent and we were cautious that this might be some sort of trap. We continued toward the building, carefully stepping over spent bullet casings and dark red blood stains. There were pieces of human remains that dogs and cats were foraging for.

They were once family pets and now were strays searching for their owners as tidbits of food, often licking their blood from the ground. Red was once my favorite color, but I had come to detest it. Blood was smeared all over the sidewalks, serving as evidence of the Jews shot in cold blood.

I noticed a tiny doll in the gutter that must have once been clutched by a little girl. Now, it was covered with her blood.

"We have to be strong, let's get inside. It's more dangerous out in the open with these bastard Nazi gunmen patrolling the streets. We need to find a place for the night, and possibly to find some food," my Pappa said.

As we entered an apartment, we could smell the stale aroma of cooking and frying food that accumulated over the years. It spawned memories of my Mamma making potato latkes at Hanukkah and baking sponge cake for Passover.

I was overcome with the eerie feeling of walking into a stranger's empty home.

There were photographs of their family everywhere. Children finely dressed up with their parents, possibly going to synagogue or a friend's home for a holiday. There were the wedding pictures of the parents, and also a metal menorah which was lying on the floor. Someone has clearly stepped on it in an attempt to destroy it.

The apartment seemed as if the occupants had their dinner interrupted by Nazi soldiers hauling them away. Five plates of rancid soup with spoons still in them were left on the table. Half eaten pieces of stale bread with butter on tiny plates and glasses of stagnant water too.

I saw a wash tub that still had powdered soap in the water that was left soaking.

My sister began scouring the kitchen for some food, as I stood there as a guest in a stranger's home, afraid to touch anything out of respect for another person's property.

I thought maybe they were coming back at any moment, and what would they say if they found us making use of their home?

My sister found some sugar packets which she put in her pocket and some stale bread.

My father made a place for us to sleep and we sat quietly eating the stale bread with rancid butter and water. The Nazis cleverly cleaned out all the food, anticipating that we would be hungry.

The following morning we were ordered to return to the "Big Ghetto."

The gates opened and I immediately noticed it was different inside. Different in a morbid way. It was gray and ugly. Once bustling with inhabitants, there were fewer people. There was blood spatter on the walls of the buildings and pools of blood on the streets.

We quickly returned to our corner in our apartment, fearing my Mamma and little sister were part of the carnage, but I was relieved to find them lying on the floor embracing and praying to God in Yiddish.

I noticed that although all the corners were still occupied, there were less people. My Mamma sprang to her feet and hugged and kissed us.

My little sister sprang onto me and hugged me so tightly.

"Please never leave me!" she cried. My mamma was so upset, she took hold of my Pappa. Cyla and I cried. "Have you heard anything that this will soon be over? Are the Russians coming back?" she desperately pleaded for information.

My father just hugged us all in a bear-type grip and responded, "I'm sorry, Gitel, there is no news," and he began to sob as well.

My Mamma told us that gangs of Lithuanians and Nazi SS were rounding up truck-loads of Jews and brutally attacking and killing them in the streets. We all feared for our fragile lives, but thankfully we were still all together…for now.

But the German killing machine was real. No one could believe that these people could ever be such inhumane evil devils.

There is a place deep in hell for these vile dogs.

Chapter 7

Winter came and we had little warm clothing, and it was very cold. There was no heat in our building and we huddled together to try to stay warm. Jenya was always in the middle.

When we were forced out of our home, it was summer. However, my father insisted on taking his long dress coat which had a full mink collar. It was very flashy, but in the ghetto flamboyant was not allowed, and the Germans directed all the prisoners to remove any fur from their garments and turn them in.

My father walked proudly through the ghetto wearing his disfigured collarless coat, and he jokingly boasted that, "thanks to him, his mink collar contributed to the German movement!"

There was a tumult at the gate this morning as groups were sent off to do their work duty. Cyla and I were ordered not to go to the sewing house anymore and were reassigned to work at the airport. Any changes were fear-inducing since we never knew if we were exchanging our slave labor for a trip to the Ponary.

We knew nothing of the airport since it was not a place we used to travel from, but now it was a cargo and military airport. Mostly for refueling planes and bringing in supplies for the Germans.

The airport was roughly 6 miles away, and took over an hour and a half to walk to. It was a long walk, but walking was safer, at least we knew there would be no detours to Ponary if we were locked in the back of a Nazi transport truck.

Our job was to shovel gravel between the railroad ties that adjoined the airport. It was hard work and we were constantly being shouted at and terrorized by the guards.

We passed near our old neighborhood on the way to the airport. We couldn't help recognizing that our once-upon-a-time neighbors were now wearing our coats and clothing that we had left hidden in our apartment.

Who could blame them, it wasn't like they thought we would be coming back anytime soon.

The work at the airport was laborious. With the addition of the long walk back and forth, my sister and I were starting to feel the toll.

One morning Cyla had an idea. Rather than both of us taking the long walk to the airport, she suggested that I should stay "home" with my mother and little sister, and when they called my name for attendance, she would raise her hand and shout "Here!" It sounded like a great foolproof idea! I was so exhausted, and I thought how wonderful it would be to stay at our place and play with Jenya, and not have to shovel gravel all day, so I happily agreed.

That morning my sister left with the group and I stayed behind with my Mamma and Jenya.

As bad luck would have it, there was a surprise awaiting my sister and the group at the airport that day. Instead of working, they were ordered into a fenced enclosure, where they saw a cattle car train waiting. She believed the train was going to Ponary, to slaughter everyone!

My sister instantly remembered my father's words:

"If you are ever asked your age, you are 21. And if you see a train, don't get on it! Run and get away!"

Cyla made a reflex decision to run for the fence, and she desperately began climbing up the barbed wires, when suddenly gunshots began firing at her, and bullets were flying by her head.

The German barbed wire was vicious, and designed to be razor sharp and impossible to get through. A bullet passed through the back of her thigh as she reached the top of the fence and it caused her to rake her leg against the barbed wire which caught her thigh, ripping her leg wide open as she reached over the top of the fence, and she fell down 8 feet to the other side.

The flesh of her thigh was dangling and bleeding profusely as the bullets continued flying past her and vicious dogs were barking from inside the fence.

She stumbled to her feet and quickly hobbled away, searching for a place to hide. She ran into a nearby cornfield and hid in a storage shed, and then wrapped her scarf around her leg as a bandage. She laid there hiding under piles of corn stalks, waiting until dark to return to us.

As she hid there, she thought to herself, "Pappa will be so proud of me for running away from the train and not getting caught!"

But before the train left, unbeknownst to her, the Germans were diligently looking for her.

The dogs tracked her and finally sniffed her out as she was hiding in the shed. Rather than just killing her on the spot, they dragged her back to the train.

There was a Polish doctor there who stitched her up.

It was agonizing since there was no sedation or pain prevention. She was then thrown into a cattle car on the train to Estonia, with all the others.

One unique quality my sister possessed was that she knew how to turn on her charm.

Cyla had a flair for phoniness. She was the original kiss-ass and flatterer when she wanted something from someone.

She could be your best friend, shower you with complements, tell you she had surprises for you, and promise you the world. After she got what she was after, she would never follow through on anything she promised.

She modeled herself after the high society actresses we saw in the movies, how glamorous they spoke and acted. It never worked on me, though, and I always saw right through her like a crystal ball. As I said before, she was proficient in the art of lying. Many others fell victim to her, especially my little sister.

Maybe that's how Cyla saved her own life when the Nazis found her. Anyone else would have been killed on the spot. I can only imagine her wooing the Nazis for being so good looking, and so intelligent as to find her. Whatever she said, she never told me, but it probably saved her life.

Word got back to us that the people on the train had been taken to the concentration camp in Vaivara, Estonia. It was operated by Estonian auxiliaries of the Nazis. How lucky was I, that the one day they deported my group, my sister had an idea that I should stay home that day.

We were worried sick about her, though. Since we had no way of finding out if she was dead or alive.

In the opposite corner of our apartment, there was a man who was responsible for collecting all the dead bodies from wherever they sent him. He was a chatty jokester when we first met.

Since then, I watched him turn into a lifeless and empty shell of a man. He hardly spoke and certainly never had anything funny to say anymore. He would return home every night depressed with sadness and the smell of death hovered over him.

We waited anxiously for his return each night, and would immediately ask him if he had seen or recovered Cyla.

His answer was always the same. He would shake his head and say, "No, no....I didn't see her."

Approximately two weeks later, someone who had been sent back to the ghetto from Vaivara, passed my Pappa a tiny little note on a crumpled piece of paper.

It was sent by Cyla!

It said, "I'm working in a camp in Vaivara, Estonia. I'm still alive. Try not to come here. Take care of Mamma and Pappa." It was short, but at least we knew she was alive, and that's what mattered most.

Two days later the Nazi thugs and Polish police came to our building and brutally kicked us out of our corner of the apartment. It wasn't just our building, we were among hundreds of other Jews in the ghetto. There was chaos and confusion as everyone was frantic and panicking, not knowing if this was a "Clean out" or just another relocation.

There was a secret nursery that was located in the basement of a building that was used as a makeshift hospital.

There were at least 40 babies there with their mothers. To our horror, a garbage truck pulled up in front of the building and a group of despicable animals raided the room. They grabbed the screaming babies by their legs and arms, sometimes two or three at a time and flung them like dead chickens into the back of the truck with the garbage.

Some smashed their heads with clubs or they kicked them like soccer balls, their skulls cracked against their assassins' heavy boots.

The mothers were already dead in the nursery, as they put up the strongest fight to protect their babies. At least they were spared and didn't have to watch as their babies were viciously murdered. How can anyone consider these sadistic animals human beings?

It's inconceivable that a human could take pleasure from killing a baby, but they did.

We were overrun by Nazi SS, Polish police, and Lithuanian thugs as they prepared to once again herd us like animals through our once beloved streets of our beautiful city. I looked back through the gates and saw three young women lagging behind in the courtyard of the ghetto.

Suddenly, someone had thrown a hand grenade at them and in an instant the three women were blown to bits.

We were made into a spectacle as we dismally marched.

There were many of our townspeople watching as we were paraded through the city, some were visibly upset and crying for us. But there were others who were taunting us along the way, shouting, "Have a nice trip, Jew bastards!"

Some even threw rocks and animal excrement at us as we trudged on to the train station.

My Pappa would gallantly walk to the outside of us, to shield us from those animals.

I held my little sister's hand tightly, and to stop her from crying, I made up a hopscotch game with her.

As we walked, we would hop over the numerous blood stains in the street. If the blood stains were too large to hop over, I would swing her over them by her hand. That's how we now played hopscotch in Vilna, Poland.

Chapter 8

We heard the loud whistle of the steam train from a distance as we approached the train station. However, I was relieved that the train that was parked at the station was connected to dozens of cattle cars. It was surely not our train. They were probably moving cattle to feed the German troops. The comfortable passenger cars were probably coming after the cattle train left and then we would ride on that. I was only 16 and naive.

As soon as we arrived at the train station, we were brutally shoved into those cattle cars at gunpoint. We were beaten by policemen, both Lithuanian and Polish, as Nazi soldiers were overseeing things with their ferocious barking dogs.

There were many Jews who refused to get on.

They were forcibly shoved in, thrown on or beaten to death with a fierce club to the head, but rarely shot. It seems that a Jew wasn't worth wasting a bullet on.

My father saw a Lithuanian thug with a bat quickly approaching us, and he quickly helped my Mamma onto the high opening of the cattle car, then my little sister, and then me before he hoisted himself up. Before he could get on, he felt the pain across his back as he was viciously struck.

There was only one pail for relieving ourselves in the entire car, which was filled quickly then overflowed all over the floor. They kept pushing more and more people in, to the point where we were all packed in, shoulder to shoulder, and we had no way to move around, lay or even sit on the floor.

The huge cattle car door slammed shut and everyone's stress level multiplied. We were imprisoned and packed like cattle going to slaughter, and we didn't know where we were going.

There were only two small windows which were too high to look through, and people were starting to get aggressive being packed so tightly. My father did his best to keep us huddled together. We took turns holding Jenya, fearing she was so little she could get pushed to the floor and trampled.

People had no choice but to relieve themselves where they stood and we were trying to keep from standing on the sewage on the floor. We had no food or water and we were sick from the fumes, the heat, claustrophobia and not being able to move. Worst of all, we didn't know how long we would be locked up in this Nazi coffin.

It seemed like an eternity as the train rambled on. The air was unbreathable, thick with the smell of human waste and vomit. People were collapsing and passing out as the physical and mental conditions of the box car were breaking us down. Those who ended up on the floor were trampled, unless there was a family member to get them up again. Some were praying out loud and most were just crying, especially the children.

After two days the train finally stopped at the Vaivara encampment.

The cattle car doors suddenly opened and we were brutally greeted by barking dogs, both human and canine.

When the camp gates opened, I saw my sister Cyla running towards us.

It was a happy reunion and we thought that we would all be together again for a while, until they suddenly began splitting up the new arrivals.

My mother, father and my little sister were immediately pushed away and sent to another camp. Everything was happening so fast.

Cyla grabbed hold of me so tightly! I couldn't move, and I desperately tried to break away from her! I wanted to go with my Mamma, Pappa and Jenya! I tried to fight her off, but she was bigger and stronger than me!

I was in a weakened state after enduring that hellacious train ride, and within a few seconds my Mamma, Pappa and Jenya were shuffled off with a crowd and they were gone, and I was stuck with my selfish sister. I was angry. Understandably, Cyla didn't want to be alone, but selfishly she wanted what was best for her, not for me.

Once they were gone she loosened her grip and I pushed away from her. I suddenly noticed her clothes, she was still wearing the barbed wire, ripped, bloody skirt that she had on when she scrambled over the fence at the airport. It resembled shredded macaroni and her leg was still healing with some of her stitches ripped apart.

I can't tell you how angry I was, that I didn't have the strength to fight off my sister and leave with my parents and little sister! Sometimes I think I'm stupid. Why didn't I do this, or why didn't I do that, go here rather than go there.

I second guess myself constantly. But the reality is, you had to be smart, clever and courageous when dealing with the Nazis. However, with the Nazi's, it was impossible to be smart. They were meticulous with details and extremely difficult to fool.

Often I thought, even though God has turned his back on us, that things happen out of luck. I truly believe that luck has a role in our survival and maybe luck is God's will. If not, I hope that someone, maybe my Grandpa or Grandma, is watching out for me.

Not going to the airport with Cyla the day she was taken, I was incredibly lucky. I'm beginning to believe that luck is all we have now. Anyone who survives this place in hell, has to be lucky.

My first day at Vaivara, they gave me an identification number and I received a piece of bread and some soup.

Cyla hid me in the outhouse at first, then snuck me into the barracks where we slept all together on wide wooden shelves (Naress) like herring packed in a can. Three wooden tiers with no mattresses or pillows. A pail that was used for human waste was at the end of the row, which overflowed onto the floor. It was unlucky for the person who had the bunks next to the pail, because of the smell.

My sister was lucky because of her injury. She worked in the kitchen and was able to get more food than everyone else. She would sometimes sneak me some extra food too. But the consequences for getting caught smuggling food were severe. You would get beaten to the point where you couldn't sit down or sometimes even beaten to death.

I was happy that I had my tooth brush. It was all I had left of my life, and I cherished it as one would cherish a sentimental religious pendant or a wedding ring. It allowed me to retain my dignity and still feel somewhat human.

German SS Aufseherinnen (Supervisors) would come each day and gather groups to do a specific work detail. I was fortunate to have a "Good German" who was not as aggressive with us. In fact, he seemed to favor me. He would come every day and choose me and about fifteen of my friends to go out to a forest next to a large field and we would move logs.

For a break, he would allow us to roam the fringed area and pick berries to eat. This went on for a few weeks, and each day he sent us to go pick berries so we had something to eat.

However, one day there was a different look in his eye and he caressed my hair whenever he walked past me.

When it was time to go berry picking, he sent my group in one direction, and ordered me alone into a dense secluded area of the forest, and he followed a short distance behind me.

"I'll show you where I saw some big juicy berries!" he seductively stated.

I was a naive teenager and went where I was told, but suddenly I became very nervous, and I realized that I was alone and unsure of what sick thoughts were present in his mind. He wanted to get me alone and have his way with me.

My instincts took over and I made a quick turn behind a juniper tree, and ran through the brush back to the area where my friends were picking berries. Afterwards, when I returned with my friends back to the forest, the German was furious and began shouting at me!

"I told you to go there! Not where you want to go!" he blasted and pointed his finger.

"I'm sorry, but there were no more berries where you sent me, so I went to the other side with my friends," I softly replied.

"Tomorrow, when I tell you where to go, you will go there!" he shouted and charged off.

I was very nervous because if I resisted, he could just shoot and kill me and leave me in the woods to rot. Which I would have preferred, rather than let that pig touch me. I was not like some of the other women in the ghetto, who would sleep with the guards for a crumb or a special favor:

"Tomorrow I may be dead, and it won't matter anymore," I thought to myself.

When the following day came, we were once again in the woods working. I was petrified, as I feared what was ahead of me.

The German had been eyeing me all morning, and when the time came, he told the other women that they should go pick berries to the left, and he pointed to me to go to the right, to the desolate area he sent me the day before.

Once again he gave me that hungry look, and nodded me on to the right.

I wasn't going to go, and so I just dropped to the ground and sat, and I went nowhere!

He kicked me to get up, then tried hoisting me up by my arm, but I just dropped again and stayed put.

"I'm not very hungry today, so I think I'll just rest here," I stated.

A few of my friends who knew what was going on, stayed behind and began chatting with me to create a diversion.

Maybe I was stupid for being defiant, but I knew I'd rather be dead than to let that Nazi bastard touch me. He gave me an angry look of discontent, but I held my ground and told him I wasn't hungry.

His eyebrows raised and he cringed, then he noticed that the other girls had found a bountiful blackberry bush, so he marched over and joined them.

He began eyeing a more willing woman he could have.

The next day we returned to the field, but there was trouble.

An ugly, scrawny serpent, a German SS Aufseher with wire glasses had interrupted our work and spoke to our commandant. His name was Schnable. He was looking to take a group of workers to dig ditches in the field for a military purpose. Immediately my "Good German" took revenge and pointed his finger at me and the girls that stood by my side the day before, and motioned to us to go with the ugly Nazi.

He took the group and marched us into the large field abutting the forest we were working in, and was constantly shouting at us to hurry up.

When we arrived at the area we were to work, there were shovels waiting for us and he ordered us to dig trenches.

With these demons you could never be sure if you were digging a fox hole for the military, or your own grave.

By now I was used to using a shovel, and with the little food we got, we didn't have a lot of energy or ambition to kill ourselves working for the Germans' benefit.

I began to shovel in a trench, where I was told to dig, when I heard heavy footsteps charging towards me. Suddenly I felt the crack of a wooden club hit me across the back. That Nazi bastard hit me several times and knocked me down into the trench, and he continued to beat me viciously.

My friends were stunned until he turned his club on them too.

He continued on a beating spree and was brutally clubbing everyone, while yelling, "Lazy Jews! Dig faster or you will be digging your graves!"

He cracked an older woman we called Ma, across her head, and split her skull open. As she fell to the ground, stunned, he pulled out his pistol and shot her in the back of her neck.

All I could think of through the pain and violence was, "What an evil bastard we now had on us, when yesterday I was running away from the 'Good German,' and now today we are getting beaten to death."

The following day we returned to the field with the Good German, when the bastard Schnable showed up again and picked me, along with about 20 other girls to work in the woods. This time I was going to be ready.

"You're not going to beat me again, you son of a bitch!" I thought to myself. I worked hard. He paced by me several times looking for a reason to hit me, but he left me alone. Such a mean bastard.

The following morning, there was an announcement that they were looking to send people to another camp in Narva. I was the first to volunteer. I wanted to get far away from those evil German bastards as soon as possible.

Cyla, although reluctant to lose her soft job in the kitchen, came with me too. I missed my parents and Jenya and I hoped to find my family there, in Narva. I was always anxious about my Mamma, Pappa and Jenya.

I received little, if any information, other than the fact that they were at the Narva concentration camp. I hope they are there so we can all be together.

I miss my mother's touch, my father's strong hugs and my little sister's soft embrace.

Chapter 9

The group of volunteers, and some who didn't, assembled by the gate the following morning. We carried what little we had and prepared to set off for Narva.

Winter was here and it was a freezing cold day. There was a light blanket of snow on the ground.

I'm now 18, and my only possession is the sparse bit of clothes on my back and my toothbrush, which I keep in my pocket at all times.

Whenever there was some water available, I would wash my face and use my toothbrush and try to clean up; just for my own dignity.

It was hell to be in this situation. I don't understand what we did that the Germans hated us so much, and to be so brutally treated is a crime against humanity. "Clean Outs" as the Nazi's called them, continued and were actually mass exterminations, a genocide of our people. They were killing men, women and even children as a sport. Families clinging together refusing to be separated were all gunned down. There were no more "Good Germans" who had an inkling of compassion.

From now on all that I saw were bloodthirsty scum! I'm learning fast though, and I'm getting smarter each day or I won't survive, but now I pray for luck rather than to God.

We were sent off to Narva on foot, wearing wooden shoes the Germans gave us to wear. We had some warm clothes that we got from dead people. In a coat I was given, I found a stitched monogram inside. It said: "This coat belongs to: Hanna Silverman."

That coat was initially a living object that was beautiful, colorful and it defined the person who wore that coat before me. The coat went to a synagogue, to the market and maybe even a joyful wedding. Now the life of its owner is gone from it, and it's not so beautiful anymore, splattered with stains of blood all over it, but it will have a new purpose and help to keep me warm.

There were a few guards with dogs guiding us, and for the most part there was no killing along the way.

The march lasted three or four days and we slept on the ground. I made a pillow out of snow and I actually slept well. I loved the fresh air and seeing stars twinkling over me. I was somewhere else and not in hell anymore.

When we finally arrived at Narva, we were overwhelmed by its size. It was very large and totally surrounded by barbed wire. The gates were made of wood and barbed wire along the top.

There were policemen eyeballing us, as they struck their heavy bats into their hands. My parents and little sister ran to us and we hugged and kissed. It was a happy but short lived reunion. We were so happy despite the deplorable position we were in. But the guards quickly came and broke us apart, and pushed us to the barracks we were assigned to.

This camp was blatantly more brutal than Vaivara. It was common to see Jews beaten and murdered daily, but at least I was back together with my family, and that was all that was important to me now.

However, shortly after our arrival I was starting to regret the move, and my sister was angry that we left

Vaivara. This was a brutal active killing camp, and they were murdering everyone that was of no use to them on a daily basis.

There was a pompous arrogant German doctor, who every day would attend morning roll calls. At the attendance, he would walk across the rows and would point at Jews to be killed. He would briefly look you over and decide if you were going to live or die with a flick of his thumb. My father was in the line behind the row who was spared. When they stepped forward, my father joined them, avoiding the next pass of the German's finger and who he was about to choose to die.

We all went from naive city people to cunning survivalists. Whatever opportunity presented itself, you had to make a split second decision which could change your life. A left turn here, an opening there, think fast, don't hesitate, do what you have to do to stay alive.

The Nazi's put us to work digging trenches in the fields, hard labor breaking rocks with heavy hammers and packing gravel under the railroad ties to keep them sturdy.

The reality was that we were maintaining the railway tracks, so they could move Jews back and forth to and from Narva.

After several months of brutal labor at Narva, we were told we were leaving all together with my family, and deported to another camp, Kivioli.

Chapter 10

It's been four years since the Russians occupied our town.

We left Narva and walked for a few days, stopping along the way only to sleep at night.

When we arrived at Kivioli, it looked just like every other camp we've been to so far. Big gates with barbed wire, the camp surrounded by razor sharp barbed wire fencing. Rows of wooden barracks lined the area, and the blueprint of the program was the same. It was only getting worse.

Tragically, upon arriving there, I was the first to come down with Typhus fever. It quickly spread throughout the barracks and the entire camp.

We had a Jewish doctor who was taking care of us the best he could, with no supplies or medicines. He risked his life and kept the disease silent from the Germans.

Any knowledge of the outbreak would have initiated the Germans to burn the camp and everyone in it to the ground. They were terrified of catching sub-human illnesses from the Jews, and wouldn't have thought twice about killing everyone.

The disease was terrible. Burning hot fever was the predominant symptom, and no matter what, you couldn't get relief from the severe high heat and dire weakness.

I stayed in the barrack hoping to recover, or to hurry up and die. Cyla also contracted it and became severely ill. She was laying next to me on the planks of the bed shelf, naked and burning up. She was so hot, she began frantically tearing the skin off her body! The disease finally passed after a week or so.

The doctor was a hero to us for covering up the disease.

The protocol of the camp was: If there was illness in the camp, the clothing was to be sanitized. They took what little clothes I had to a laundry house.

In my recovery, I was weak and disoriented and forgot to remove my tooth brush from my skirt and when it was cleaned, the heat from the cleaning was so intense that the bristles on the tooth brush caught on fire and completely burned up my clothes and I had nothing to wear!

We were all forced into the bath house to clean up and I sat on a stool crying, with only a rag around me. The other women laughed and made fun of me for not having anything to wear. I cried and I cried, there was no one who would help me. I was so devastated that I lost the only possession I owned and I had nothing to put on. My Pappa was waiting outside for me when he heard me crying. He looked in a window and saw me sitting on the floor naked, with just a little rag covering me, as the women taunted me. He came rushing in and took hold of me, and embraced me and held me close as I cried, "Look Pappa, my clothes were burned up, and I have nothing to cover myself." I hysterically cried and cried.

He held me tightly to his body, and he began to cry too: "My child, as long as I have you!" and he held me tight and covered me with himself.

A kind woman had found some clothes and handed them to my Pappa. I was still so weak from the typhus that he carried me back to the barracks, and when I arrived, there was no place for me to lay.

There were 200 people in our barracks with 3 pails to hold human waste and the only place for me was right next to those pails! I had to lay next to them as the fumes were overwhelming. The sewage was all over the floor next to me and the air was sour with the smell of urine and feces.

I cried myself to sleep, burying my face under my arm until morning came. My father came to me and brought some potatoes for me to eat.

It was his ration for the day. But when I saw it was his only ration for the day, in my weakened state, I told him that I wasn't hungry. He replied, "I'm not hungry either, maybe I'll give these potatoes to the Lager Fuhrer (Camp commandant) for his breakfast," my father joked, and he pushed the potatoes for me to eat.

In the past, living in our apartment in Vilna, I always took potatoes for granted, now these potatoes are the best thing I could have dreamed of.

I slowly recovered and so did Cyla. Sadly, the Lager Fuhrer found out that the Jewish doctor had hidden the Typhus fever from him and had him assassinated in front of the entire camp the following morning. He was a true hero though, and he saved countless lives.

Chapter 11

It was difficult to keep track of months and days, although there was always someone who made it their job to keep track of such things. I know it was the winter of 1944 and I was 19 years old. The orders came from the Lager Fuhrer that a large group of Jews were being moved out. My family and I were leaving Kivioli and going back to Viavara. I was in a group, separated from my family, while we all marched back to Viavara in the frigid cold. Being outside of the encampments was like a holiday for us. Breathing fresh air, sleeping on the snow and not working was a relief. However, while we were sleeping outside, there were several women with us who had long hair.

We made pillows of snow for our heads to rest on as we slept. When the temperature dropped through the night, their hair froze into their pillows of solid ice and snow. When they tried to get up in the morning, they desperately struggled and couldn't get up, their hair was completely frozen to the ground. Rather than cut their hair from the ice, the Nazis just shot them all dead and left them there.

When we finally arrived at Viavara, the Germans wasted no time dividing everyone and redirecting them to different camps. Viavara was like a distribution camp. They sent slaves to where labor was needed or just off to be killed if they were of no use to them.

I found my Mamma with Jenya and my Pappa was with Cyla. We were there for one hour. Kissing and hugging and crying that we were all together. We learned that we were being sent to Ereda, a camp not far from Viavara, in Estonia.

The train depot was near the camp gates and suddenly there was a German voice blasting on a loudspeaker:

"Attention Juden. Due to the frigid weather, deep snow and the long walk for the children, we have arranged for a special train to take the youngsters to Ereda. Only children are allowed. You will rejoin them when you arrive in a few days."

I told my Mamma and Pappa that Jenya should go on the train with the other kids. The walk would be too much for her to survive.

Jenya began to get upset. She did not like the idea of being separated from any of us, even if it meant taking a train ride to spare her from freezing to death.

There was a group of Jews that they were preparing to depart for Ereda by foot. I begged Jenya to get on the train, and that I would go with the group and be right behind her.

I told her with deepest compassion and sincerity: "I will meet you there in a few days and after that, we will be together forever, my Jeningka!" Reluctantly, she agreed and I took her by her little hand and put her on the train. Immediately, I rushed over to the departing group and I edged my way in with them. It was risky because there was an assigned amount of people in the group. Since I forced my way in, someone was pushed out. But no one said a word.

My Parents and Cyla stayed behind and would leave when they were told.

The big gate opened and my group of about 80 people headed through the snow covered ground and out through the ominous gates. I had no time for hugs, kisses or goodbyes.

I couldn't take a chance and wander away from the group, risking my opportunity to leave.

I promised Jenya I would meet her, and I was determined to fulfill my promise.

Then suddenly, as I walked out through the gate, I felt something tear apart inside of me! It was as if someone threw a lightning bolt into my chest! Whether it was something physical or mental, I do not know. Whatever it was, it came out of nowhere from somewhere, and a very strong feeling of grief overwhelmed me. It was so severe blood actually began dripping from my nose. I wouldn't turn around to wave goodbye to my parents. For if they saw me bleeding, they would become alarmed and run to me, and possibly be shot and killed.

Instead, I picked up a handful of snow and pressed it under my nose to soak up the blood. I pressed on with the group. Trudging through the bitter cold while only wearing wooden shoes on my feet. The only thing that motivated me was seeing my little Jeningka again, and to hold and kiss her, and be with her forever as I had promised her.

I thought how difficult the trek through the snow would have been for her, and all the other children who were on the train. This was the first sign of compassion I had ever seen by the Germans. Maybe things would be better in Ereda. I hoped she would be okay until I could be reunited with her again.

We traveled for days until finally the gates of Ereda were in view. I was cold and tired. We had nothing to eat and only snow to drink. The thought of being with my little sister kept me going. I was so excited to be reunited with Jenya, I didn't feel that my feet were frozen.

As we approached the encampment something didn't seem right. It was dark and lifeless. There was no one around. In fact the camp was completely empty, and my group was the first to arrive.

There were no children, just a few guards who began shouting at us to form a line. I started to panic, desperate to find Jenya!

"Where are the children who were sent to Erida on the train from Viavara?!" I anxiously asked a guard.

He laughed at me and said: "This is not Erida," and he pushed me away. I was devastated that my little sister and all the other children were not here!

I promised Jenya that I would come to her. She is waiting for me and she is alone! At some point through our travels, the Nazis changed our destination and we were not going to Erida.

I fell to the ground, and I had no words. I was overwhelmed with tears of grief. I didn't know where my little sister was and I broke my promise to be with her. I cried uncontrollably for days.

Chapter 12

There was nothing I could do except pray that my parents arrived at some point to Erida and Jenya was with them.

Immediately, we were put to work. I was all alone and did what I had to do. I lost track of my little sister and only God knew if my parents and Cyla were with her.

After a few months working at this small camp, there was an announcement that we were going to be moving to Erida! I was so excited at the thought that I'll finally be with my little sister! A few days earlier, I had found a piece of hard candy that a guard must have dropped and I hid it. I wanted to save it, to give to Jenya when I got to be with her. We left the camp in a group, and once again it was cold with deep snow on the ground.

I didn't care what the conditions were, I only cared that in a few days I would finally be together with my darling little Jenya.

It was late at night when we arrived at Erida. I'll never forget the big green gates that were beginning to open up when we arrived. The Jewish prisoners and guards were inside watching me. I was so anxious to see my little sister.

As cold and tired as I was, with all my might and strength, I ran into the camp. I saw a Jewish woman standing near the gate and I ran to her. "Where are the kids?! Where are the kids?!!" I impatiently shouted. She looked confused.

"What kids are you talking about?" she replied.

"The kids that came here on the train from Viavara!"

The woman bowed her head solemnly and lowered her voice: "Those children were all killed two weeks ago."

I was stunned and I couldn't comprehend her words!

"I don't believe you! It's a lie!!" I cried out and I shook her. "Where are they buried if this is true?!"

The woman pointed to a large mound covered with fresh dirt in the rear of the encampment.

I let go of the woman, and ran as fast as I could to the barren hill of dirt!

"Jenya, Jenya, I am here for you! I came to be with you, just as I promised! Where are you? Where are you!! Please answer me, Jenya!!!" I screamed, and screamed with all the strength I had left. But there was no answer...just darkness and silence.

I fell onto the mound of freshly packed earth, clawing the dirt and crying uncontrollably for my little sister.

I feared that she was pushed into the trench and buried alive, since it was more important to the Germans to save a bullet than the mercy of a quick death for a Jewish child. I was sick with fear. Was she killed before they buried her, or was she buried alive with all the other children by those cold blooded, heartless monsters.

I cried until I had no more salt for tears left in my body. A group of women who had also lost their children had heard me wailing on the grave mound, and they came to see me. Their eyes were filled with grief and sadness. They encircled me and wrapped their arms around me, engulfing me in an embrace. "She was only 9 years old! Just a little girl and they murdered her! Where is our God?!!" I cried.

The women were silent but their embrace spoke more powerfully than their words. We were all affected by these murderous demons, and at any time they saw fit, we could be next.

The following morning the women showed me the little animal hut where Jenya slept.

There were dozens of rows of tiny arched top huts which were open ended and only tall enough to slide in and sleep.

Much like something a chicken or goose might seek for shelter to get out of the rain.

Jenya had no blanket or pillow, and slept in freezing temperatures, on the frozen ground alone, with only what she was wearing when she left us. I crawled inside and found strands of her fine black hair that had been frozen to the ground, and a small can of meat hidden under a tuft of grass. She must have found it at some point. Jenya was much like me, and she must have hidden it to share with me when I arrived.

I carefully extracted the few strands of Jenya's fine black hair from the ground and braided it into a short piece of string. I held the braided hair in my hand and smelled her scent as I held it tightly against my cheek. I kissed it and I held it dear to me. It was all that I had left of my dear little sister. I blamed myself; Jenya was dead because I told her to go on the train.

She didn't want to go, but because I promised her that I would be there with her, she reluctantly got on the train. "Why didn't I go with her on the train? Maybe they would have let me go along with her!"

Again, I think about the choices I could have made. After all the lies the Nazis told us, why would anyone believe they would do a kind act such as help the children along with a train ride.

I alone carry the guilt of my little sister's death. She trusted me to keep her safe and now she was dead because of me. I'll never forgive myself.

Chapter 13

I torture myself about Jenya's death every day. Other than hate and despise the animals who murdered her, I blame myself for forcing her onto the train. I had no contact with my family for a long time, and didn't know where they were or if they were still alive.

They weren't at Erida and we were all lied to about where we were supposedly going that day back when we arrived in Viavara. Only the children were going to Erida by train and it was an evil scheme by the Nazis to separate the children from their families so they would be easier to kill.

The Germans had us working, digging ditches and camouflaging bridges to conceal them from being bombed from the allied forces.

We worked every day and were supervised by Aufsehers who were usually lower ranked personnel.

One particular day, we were digging trenches near the forest fringe when suddenly I got a cramp in my belly. I was feeling ill from the spoiled soup they gave us to eat the night before. I felt my belly was trying to expel the bad food and I had to go to the woods to relieve myself immediately. There were no Aufsehers close by, so I just slipped into the cover of the bushes and relieved myself without permission.

When I came out, an Aufseher saw me and asked me where I had been, since I had no permission to leave.

I began to tell him I had stomach cramps and urgently had to relieve myself.

He seemed to be fine with that.

However, the Arbeiten (work) Fuhrer who was in charge of the overseers came charging over to see why I was talking to the guard. His name was Schmidt. He was a short, round-faced creep with tiny scrawny chicken arms.

He privately conversed with the guard then turned his attention to me. He charged over and aggressively grabbed me by my shirt and ruffed me up!

"How old are you?" he shouted at me.

I replied as my father had taught me even though I was only 19. "I'm 21," I nervously stated.

"You're not 21! You look like you are 15! When we return to the camp, the Lager Furher (camp commandant) will give you 21 sticks across your ass for talking to your Aufseher!" he screamed at the top of his lungs with his shrieking voice.

The threat of 21 was a death sentence and I felt as if I was punched in the stomach. I was so scared that I would never survive the 21 cracks from the Lager Fuhrer's club and would be killed that night.

I continued to work, thinking, "Well, whatever is going to happen will happen."

When I returned to the camp, all the guards who worked for the Lager Furher miraculously disappeared. I was well liked amongst them, and no one wanted to be the one to receive the order to beat me to death. When I went to my barracks, the women there had heard the bad news and were terrified for me.

It was as if I had a death sentence placed upon my head.

I had a fond relationship with my barrack mates, and they were tossing out ideas to save myself, such as to put a pillow or rags under my clothes to soften the blows of the Lager Furher's club.

However, I am a stubborn person and I have my dignity.

I refused to lower myself to those Nazi bastards, and I would not let them break me. There was word that a boy who they found smuggling a piece of bread into the camp also had a date with the Lager Furher and his club tonight as well.

A male Jew who was the liaison between the Lager Furher and the prisoners entered our barracks and reported, "The Lager Fuhrer doesn't feel like hitting tonight because he is too drunk."

I was so relieved since I felt that maybe it will just be forgotten.

However, about an hour later the same Jewish liaison returned to our barracks and called out my number, and so I came forward. "The Lager Fuhrer decided he should fulfill his duty, and give the beatings tonight," he somberly stated.

The women of my barracks perked up again, begging me to put a pillow on my bottom! They were so worried about me, but I took a deep breath and I dreadfully followed the liaison back to the Lager Fuhrer's office.

The liaison knocked on the door, and the Lager Furher called out to enter. He sat at his desk with his tall black boots, pressed uniform and greased down black hair. His German military hat was carefully positioned on his desk. He held his ominous club in his hand, ready to kill. My heart was pounding just like a mouse in the claws of a cat.

He spoke to me. "Take off your hat," he ordered.

I removed my hat, and he squinted at me as he looked me over.

"Hmmmph, A real Jewish type," he smugly stated.

"Tell me what happened?" he questioned.

I stood tall and replied, "If I tell you, will you believe me?!"

The liaison became nervous since it appeared I was being disrespectful to Lager Furher and shushed me.

"You won't believe me anyways!" I exclaimed.

"Just tell me what happened, Feisty girl," he calmly stated.

The liaison glared at me, begging me to settle down with his eyes.

I took a deep breath and I spoke,

"We were near the forest digging ditches when I had an emergency. I am not complaining about the gourmet food we get, but something I ate made me ill and I suddenly had stomach cramp pains and I felt I had to urgently relieve myself. I looked for someone to ask, but there was no one around to ask permission for me to go. I quickly went into the woods and relieved myself. It was less than a minute that I was gone. When I immediately came back to work, the Aufseher asked me where I was, and I told him I had a diarrhea emergency. However, there was no one there to ask permission. Had I waited, I would have soiled myself, and no one would be happy with that since there is no place to clean up. Herr Schmidt, saw me explaining to my boss and he didn't like it."

The Lager Furher intently listened, as he leaned back in his chair and stared at me. He was watching my eyes to see if I would look away from his searing gaze. He abruptly stood up from his desk and gripped his hideous club. I closed my eyes, and my knees began to get weak. Instantly, I began to sweat and I was losing my breath.

He took his club and swung it toward me, pointing toward the door.

"Go on, Feisty. Get out of here. Go back to your barracks."

The liaison was so overwhelmed he began to cry and thanked The Lager Furher for his compassionate decision, and we left together.

When we returned to the barracks, he entered before me with a look of despair and shook his head with sadness that it was bad news.

Everyone in the barracks was standing and waiting for me to return. Some were already crying, no one thought it was going to be good. I was very much liked by my barrack mates, and they were so worried about me.

When I entered the barracks, I strolled in dancing and they saw I was perfectly fine!

They were in shock and overwhelmed with joy that I was unscathed, and still alive for that matter.

They all grabbed me, and hugged and kissed me to no end. I suppose I was a hero that night since I wouldn't sink down to try to protect myself, and my dignity was an inspiration to them all.

I later heard that the boy who had been caught with a piece of bread was also granted a stay of punishment. Lucky for us, the Lager Furher wasn't in the mood or too drunk to beat anyone that night.

In the following days I went to work, Schmidt (who was disappointed that I was still alive) was constantly watching me, lying in wait for me to do something wrong.

I think he was upset that he tried to get me a beating of 21, but when the Larger Fuhrer believed me over him, it made him look like a fool.

It was comical as he hopped around like a humpty dumpty, shrieking orders at everyone as he flapped his chicken arms erratically.

One morning, I had to look away to hide my face as he was carrying on, so he wouldn't see me laughing at him. I didn't know he was watching me at that moment since he was shouting at someone else, but because he was always watching me and waiting for me to make a mistake, he caught me laughing at him.

He rushed over to me and began brutally punching me until I fell down to the ground. Then he would give me a few fierce kicks for good measure.

This pattern went on for some time. Whenever I showed up for work he was looking for me, and he would charge over and start punching me with his feeble arms. I was constantly bruised up and in pain afterwards.

I think he realized he didn't measure up as a higher level Nazi and was frustrated that he was a poor excuse of one, so he took it out on me.

"You go to hell," I whispered to myself as he hit me.

Soon, an opportunity arose where they were looking for volunteers to leave Erida for a satellite camp. I jumped at the opportunity to get away from that bastard Schmidt.

There was always a risk of changing camps. It could be worse, but there was always a chance that I could reunite with my parents and Cyla. I was fearful they didn't know that Jenya was killed after I was the one to convince her to go on the train.

My parents will be devastated, and Cyla will probably remind everyone that I was the one who made her get on the train. She was right, and now I have to carry that guilt with me for the rest of my life.

Chapter 14

The following morning, we were told that we were leaving and instructed to gather our things, which was nothing really.

I kept the sacred can of meat for my Mamma and Pappa, just in case I found them.

My barrackmates were sad to see me go, but they understood that I had to get away from Schmidt and hopefully find my family.

We walked for about two days until we arrived at the camp which had no name that I can remember.

Surprisingly, there was a nurse there that lived on my block in Vilna and she knew my family well.

There were a few Jewish boys who were bringing supplies back and forth between several camps. One of the boys had left a note with the nurse. When she saw me, she was so excited and showed me the note. It was from my father! He was asking her if she had seen his Rochelka and little Jenya. He lost track of them and he is very worried.

The nurse promptly wrote back a note that I was with her, and she sent it back with the boys! I was excited because my father was nearby, but I didn't know how he would endure the fact that Jenya had been killed. I was afraid he would justly blame me. I knew my sister Cyla would stoke the fire, and they would be devastated. I decided to tell them in person what I had done.

The nurse introduced me to two men who traveled back and forth to the nearby camp where my father was. I asked them if they could take me to work so I could possibly see my Pappa.

They were hesitant to take me alone. However, if I could get four more women to go, it would be safer.

The following morning the two men, and four of my friends, traveled to the area where they were working.

I was excited that I might get to see my Pappa and be held by him once again! Were in the middle of a large field, and we were brought to a dispatch area to assign work, where scores of other women were already gathered.

There was a heavy set German who was in charge of assigning work (Arbeits Auftraggeber) to the work groups. His name was Hassmann.

When he looked us all over, pondering what we would be suited for. He stated: "Whoever is cold, come clean my trailer."

Dozens of women naively jumped up and volunteered, "I'm cold! I'm cold!" they begged.

I was smart by now, and knew that the German was not just looking for someone to clean his trailer. So I stayed back and acted disinterested. He noticed me trying to hide behind the women and he shouted to me: "Hey Blackie!" referring to my black hair. "You come clean my trailer!"

I was not prepared for this. I just wanted to find my Pappa, not to be a play thing for this dog. He turned and entered his trailer, and I was forced by a guard to follow him in. He sat down at a small table and began stuffing his face with buttered bread and crudely spooning up a large bowl of beef soup into his fat face, as he slumped over with his elbows firmly planted on the table. I immediately began to tidy up things and he started to ask me questions, "What's your name, Blackie?"

"My name is Rochela Bolber."

"How old are you?" he questioned with his mouth stuffed full of food.

"21," I replied.

"Where did you live before the war?" he carelessly asked.

"Vilna," I replied.

I kept my answers brief, since it made me sick to be in his presence. Maybe he was there when they killed my little sister. If he wasn't, he was still a Nazi son of a bitch. But I had to become an actress, if not for any reason but to survive. If I could have gotten away with killing him I would have done it in a second. But my goal was to find my Mamma, Pappa and Cyla.

I told him that my Pappa was at the nearby camp, and I am hoping to reunite with him.

"Oh, we are going there every day," he slobbered through his soup.

"Can I come along with you?" I matter of factly questioned as I began sweeping the floor.

He knew that it would mean a lot to me for me to see my father, and he began to toy with me.

"If I say no, will you cry?" he smirked.

"No…. I won't cry," I stated.

He stopped eating his soup and let out a noxious burp, and seemed to ponder.

"Well, you can come if you want," he arrogantly stated, and then he pushed the remaining soup in his bowl across the table towards me.

"Here, eat!" and offered me his spoon.

I tensed up, because I knew that if I accepted his offer, there was something I would have to do in return. I wanted to see my Pappa so badly, but I would not sacrifice my dignity and be used as a plaything for that filthy pig.

"No thank you, I'm not hungry," I firmly stated.

Hassmann was bewildered and stared at me. Then he stood up, and he walked to the door with the half-eaten soup bowl.

He opened the door and shouted out, "Who is hungry?"

Everyone trampled over themselves, rushing over for the possibility of getting a spoonful of soup.

He turned back to me. "How come you are not hungry? It seems everyone else you came with is."

"I have enough," I replied.

He nodded me out and brought a different woman into the trailer. I was relieved and rushed over to the men who brought us.

They said we were all leaving at noon to go to my Pappa's camp. I was so excited! I had the can of meat that I had been saving, hidden under my hat. As hungry as I was, never did it cross my mind to eat the can of meat. I knew my Mamma and Pappa needed it more than me.

They put us all on a truck and we went to the camp. It was a treat to ride after all the walking we usually had to do.

When we arrived at the camp, I searched everywhere for my Pappa, but they were out of the camp doing labor. I asked a pleasant looking guard if he knew my Pappa. He replied:

"Yes, we all know your Pappa, Yeruchim. He constantly begs us in a friendly way, 'Please bring me my daughter, bring my daughter Rochelka to me....'

"The guards then asked, 'Who is your daughter?'"

"And he says, 'She will be the most beautiful girl you have ever seen!'"

I blushed and felt a warmth from hearing my father's words from the German.

"Your Pappa loves you very much, and he was right. You are the most beautiful girl," the soldier said.

We had to leave and so I asked the guard if he would give the can of meat to my Pappa, and he gladly said he would.

Days later, my sister Cyla wrote me a note.

"They received the meat from the guard but they were still starving." She asked me if I could send more food.

I was happy to hear that they got the meat. I was starving too, but I had to help my Mamma and Pappa.

Our daily ration was a third of a loaf of bread cut into three slices for morning, noon and night.

I would get one loaf for three people and I gave up my ration for three days so that I could save a loaf of bread for my family. I scavenged up some sour oatmeal which was putrid and I ate it for three days. I had nothing else to eat.

I asked one of the men who was traveling each day to my father's camp to bring him the bread, and he took it for me and gave it to him.

One thing that you could be sure of…when someone made a promise to you, they would honor their word. A person's promise was more trustworthy than anything, since in those times a handshake was like a written agreement and no one wanted to be known as a dishonest deal breaker.

Chapter 15

A few weeks had passed and I still never got the opportunity to be with my family.

This morning I noticed a lot of activity happening around us in the camp. Guards were getting ready for something big, and that sort of thing always made everyone extremely nervous. I was hoping we were moving to my Pappa's camp.

During roll call that morning, the Lager Fuhrer made an announcement:

"Prepare to move out tomorrow morning. Most everyone in the area is being relocated from Estonia back to Poland. You are one of the lucky ones traveling to Stutthof, one of our more modern and accommodating work camps."

Everyone began to chatter and panic, because everyone had heard of Stutthof. Not only was it a slave labor camp, but it was also a killing camp.

Although there were always individualized killings in the camps we all had been in, none of them were mass extermination camps like Stuthoff.

The following morning, we began a march towards the coast of the Baltic sea where we were herded into a seaport freight yard and loaded onto ships. In the yard, I faintly heard someone enthusiastically shouting my name. "Rochelka! Rochelka!" It was my Mamma!

They were also being relocated to Stuthoff and at last, I was reunited with my Mamma, Pappa and Cyla.

It was a happy reunion and we passionately held and kissed each other.

"Where is Jenya?!" my father anxiously questioned. Suddenly, he saw my demeanor deflate and my face went pale.

I took a heavy breath. "They killed all the children on the train, Pappa. The group I left with was diverted to a different camp without my knowledge, and I couldn't get to her! I was two weeks too late before I was able to get to Erida. I searched for her immediately, but they told me that the Germans had already killed all the children."

"No, no, no, no!!!" my Mamma shrieked as she clutched her hair with both hands ripping pieces out of her head.

My father grabbed hold of my Mamma and held her tightly so she couldn't hurt herself. He lost his wind and couldn't breathe while tears poured from his eyes. My sister Cyla was in shock but didn't say anything.

"It is my fault! I made her take the train, not knowing that she would be in danger! I promised her that I would be with her forever and I failed her!" I cried.

My Pappa pulled me in close with his embrace with my Mamma, and we all cried together. "Don't blame yourself, you wanted to help her, and no one could imagine such evil bastards could exist to murder children," he struggled to say.

We stood there and wept and held each other for some time. Other prisoners passed by staring at us. I saw them looking and thought, to them this is just another day in hell. To my family, it was the end of our lives with the death of my little sister.

At some point we were ordered to board a freight ship that was not designed for moving people, just freight. My parents were still crying and visibly upset over Jenya, and now a piece of us was gone forever. Sadly, we weren't alone since most everyone on the ship had pieces of their loved ones missing from them as well. I didn't know how to go on, it just seemed inevitable that we are all destined to be murdered once we are all used up by these Nazi vermin.

The ship was full beyond capacity. There were not many places to sit or sleep except on the floors. The guards watching us were complacent and we were able to move around the boat freely. I suppose they weren't too worried, it's not like anyone was going to run away.

There was some chatter that the Allies were bombing Germany, and that the Germans were losing the war.

We were all hopeful that the war would soon come to an end, but for us it couldn't come soon enough.

One Jewish man jokingly suggested that we offer the captain of the ship a dozen eggs to take us to America. "Oh America," it was such a faraway place for me. I wondered if the people there even knew our plight.

Was there even a remote possibility that I would ever live to see America? I could only dream of it.

I visualized the Statue of Liberty from seeing pictures of it in my books. A place where we could all be free, and not have to worry about being killed because of who we were. I began to cry, believing that America was a dream that would never come true for me.

We sailed off and the first evening at sea, my father slipped out of our compartment. He said he was going for a walk.

He looked terribly sad and I followed him, stealthily staying out of his sight. He walked up to the front of the ship's bow, clenching his hands onto the deck railing. He was in a daze as he was staring out at the sea. I watched him from a short distance and I saw him contemplating something in his mind. He softened his grip on the railing and so I moved over to him as he continued to blindly gaze out at the water. He felt my presence as I was standing next to him, and I put my hand on top of his.

"I want to be with her, Rochelka. Jenya is alone and scared. I feel that I want to go and be with her in heaven. I've lost one third of my soul, and I don't want to live anymore. I want to go right now, I don't want her to be alone and she needs me," and he began to lift his leg over the railing.

I grabbed onto him, pulling him back onto the ship's deck!

"But I need you! And Mamma and Cyla need you too, Pappa!" I cried.

"I love you so much, Rochel. But I can't live if a piece of my heart is mutilated. Take care of your Mamma and Cyla," he whispered.

I clenched onto his body and wouldn't allow him to lift his leg from the railing. "Please Pappa! I'm begging you not to do this! It's my fault Jenya is dead! I was the one that made her get on the train, and I was the one who promised her that I would meet with her and be with her forever. It should be me that goes to her, not you!"

And so I started to quickly climb over the railing! I could feel the cool breeze of the watery mist from the ship's bow cutting its course through the black water. Now my Pappa was grabbing hold of me, trying to hold me back!

"Let me go, she is all alone, Pappa!" I shouted.

My father frantically grabbed at me and pulled me back. "I won't lose my Rochelka, too! It was not your decision to make her go on the train. I was there too, and I could have said no! I'm the Pappa, and I felt as you did, that she never would have survived the walk in the deep snow and freezing cold. I was a fool to believe that the Germans would actually have compassion for the children and let them ride on the train rather than walk. We all pushed her to go! No one had a crystal ball and sadly Jenya paid the price. But you are right, now we need each other! There is time for us to be together later. For now let's just survive, and not let these evil bastards take everything from us!"

He held me tightly and I reached into my pocket and took out the piece of braided string I made from Jenya's hair. I gently placed it into my Pappa's hand. "This is all we have left of her," I cried through my tears. He took the hair and lifted it to his face and kissed it.

Then he cupped his hands over the fine strands and he began desperately inhaling it, trying to smell her essence in a way to bring her back to him, just one more time. We both wept, but there was such an enormous hole left in our lives without little Jenya. It would be so difficult to overcome. We held each other as we walked back to the cabin.

My Mamma was grieving in her own way, trying to hide her sorrow and burying her tears. We weren't the only ones who lost loved ones. There were horrific events transpiring everyday.

After two days at sea, we arrived at the seaport where we were harshly unloaded. Polish policemen with sticks and Nazi's with threatening barking dogs lunged at us as they chased us off the boat.

We were walking across a sandy beach when I stepped on something round and hard under the sand. I knelt down and dug it up, it was a dried up prune. It was hard as a rock, but I wanted to share it with my parents and Cyla. We each took a quarter of a bite. It was nice to taste something other than bread, but that's all it was, a taste. We hadn't eaten for days since there was no food on the ship.

But at least there was no killing and we were all together now.

We began our trek, walking to Stuthoff. Four hundred people marched through the small oceanside village to the death camp.

When we arrived, the big barbed wire gates methodically began to slowly swing open.

We were all well aware that those gates were known as the Gates of Death. We were marched in as the resident prisoners silently gazed at us, bowing their heads as if they were trying to tell us that we had just passed into someplace worse than hell.

The camp appeared typical, much like some of the other camps I was in, only much bigger.

Guards with machine guns and dogs, walking skeletons dressed in rags and lost souls wandering about with the look of hopelessness in their faces was all the same.

There was something different about this place, though. Big tall chimneys billowing out smoke and the noxious smell of burning meat was in the air.

Once we were inside the camp, the men and women were separated and we were told that we were being sent to the showers, to be disinfected and washed.

I was with my Mamma and Sister, and my Pappa was sent off with the men. It was frightening since we were forced to strip naked and enter the large shower chamber. The three of us stood naked in that room, shaking with fear, along with two-hundred other naked and terrified women.

It was a killing chamber where thousands before us were murdered with Zyklon B, a hydrogen cyanide poison gas.

Most died a horrific death, struggling not to breathe the burning gas into their lungs until they succumbed. But there were others that would still be alive when the gas was cleared and the doors opened. They were shot in the back of the neck and finished off.

A group of prisoners had the horrific job of dragging out the dead bodies, shearing the men and women's hair off, and removing any gold dental work or Jewelry before dumping the bodies into mass burial pits or burning them in the ovens.

The Nazis sold off giant bales of the Jewish victims' hair to fabric and electronic factories for pennies per kilogram. Some of the items fabricated from the hair can still be found in German homes today.

All of us were silently staring up at the water nozzles, some crying, all praying for water to come out and not the poison gas, which often did. Suddenly, we heard the pipes begin to jolt and ice cold water came shooting out of the nozzles, glorious ice cold water and not the gas!

We were able to shower and I noticed there were some hot pipes behind me giving off heat. I accidentally bumped into a pipe with my arm and got a severe burn, scalding my skin.

I was afraid to tell anyone because it could turn into a bad situation, and keeping quiet was always a safer thing to do.

After the shower they herded us all into a big barracks, with a wooden plank floor. There were no bunk shelfs, just a big empty room for 200 women.

That's when we were viciously beaten and slapped by a group of all female guards who were our new German Aufensehers. They barked at us to lie on the floor, shut up and sleep. This was our introduction to the sadistic and maniacal Blitz Fraus (Lightning women) of Stuthoff.

Since the German war effort was failing, male Nazi guards were redirected from the concentration camps to the Russian front.

The Nazis recruited uneducated women who had menial jobs such as driving trolleys or working on farms to work as camp guards for pay.

Some had been Hitler Jungen (Hitler's maniacal version of the boy and girl scouts), who were brainwashed and indoctrinated into the Nazi SS ideology as young children. Most regarded Hitler and Nazis to a higher degree than their own parents and would sometimes report their families to authorities as not being devout Nazis.

These women, who were mostly in their early twenties, were a group of the most viciously brutal and savage women, with the job of making our lives miserable. With two-hundred women in the room, there was obviously going to be chatter. The Blitz Fraus were sadistically walking around the room with pails of ice cold water, and if they heard someone speaking they would douse us to keep us quiet. My sister and I laid on top of Mamma so that she would remain dry, but at 4 am they made us go outside for a roll call. Stuthoff was situated at a difficult location.

The nights were freezing cold and the days were sweltering hot. We spent hours being soaking wet and freezing cold. The three of us were huddling together, desperately trying to stay warm.

The Lager Fuhrer finally came out of his building and stood erect as the Blitz Fraus slapped us hard as they counted us. When one of the Blitz Fraus came to my row, she suddenly stopped in front of me, and stared at me.

"How old are you!" she barked.

She was extremely mean spirited and frightening to me.

"I'm 21," I replied.

"You are 21?!!! You are a lying Jew! You are a child and should be with the little Jew shits who are good for nothing!" she shouted and grabbed hold of my arm.

My heart sank as I knew "a good for nothing Jew" wasn't useful to them, and it meant I would end up like my little sister. Suddenly an officer appeared and approached her with a ledger book. He was confused and needed her help to figure out why the calculations in the ledger were not adding up. She let go of me and began intently looking in the book. She became so engaged with the officer, that she suddenly walked away with him and forgot about me!

This is the luck I was sometimes blessed with. Someone must be watching over me. It was a miracle that I survived that moment.

Later in the day, they gave us some soup made of grass and water in a tin bowl. I always tried to be clean and didn't want to use my dirty hands to eat. I had found a stick on the ground, and used it as a fork to eat the grass. A Blitz Frau took notice of me using the stick as a more civilized way to eat my grass, and wanted to demean me in front of everyone. She kicked the bowl of soup on me, and it spilled all over myself. She laughed at me and walked on.

There were some male Nazi guards in Stutthof and they were all cold-blooded bastards, but even worse than them were the Blitz Frau women. They tortured us not only physically, but mentally.

Every morning we were allowed to use the washroom to clean ourselves. The room was only big enough for six people at a time. They controlled the water flow.

Once you entered the room, you only had a few seconds to soap up your hands and wash with water. But they would watch us, and shut off the water before we could rinse the soap off. One morning, I decided I was going to be ready and out smart them.

I'll use a tiny amount of soap and then quickly wash my hands! But the Blitz Fraus were smarter than that, and they chased me out with a bat before I could ever wash the soap off. That's how they punished us. Not being able to wash the soap off our hands was a problem because of the lye in the soap. If you rubbed your eyes, it would burn and it was uncomfortable once it dried up.

For supper, it was always the same soup made from just water and grass. I recognised the grass immediately when I first saw it in our soup. It was called Pokshera, blister grass. It had sharp blades and would cut you if you rubbed against it in a field.

The Nazis wouldn't ever consider using just plain grass, because it would be more punishment to serve us blister grass.

The metal bowls they gave us had a stamped bottom which resembled a lid of a Jar. There was always a few tablespoons of soup left at the bottom of the bowl, which as bad as it was, was better than nothing. The Blitz Fraus would walk past us and throw fistfuls of sand in our bowls to destroy whatever soup was left and prevent us from eating it.

They started making us work right away. My father always told us to work, and if we had the chance to slip away we should meet in Vienna. I don't think he really expected that we would all escape, but it was an uplifting thought.

Our work was usually the same, digging ditches, carrying wood in the forest and knocking the stones in between the railroad ties.

We had a German Aufseher who took a liking to me. He once offered me a piece of the sandwich he was devouring. I refused to eat it since I was too proud to take food that had been previously eaten, no matter how hungry I was, especially from a Nazi. On our way to work, we often walked through the village and passed restaurants with their garbage cans piled high with food scraps.

The Aufseher would allow our group of women to garbage pick and scavenge for any morsels of food. When he noticed that I refused to eat from the garbage cans, he surprised me one day with a fresh and complete ham sandwich. Even though it wasn't kosher, I couldn't refuse it. He saw that I was different, and he was impressed that I wouldn't belittle myself by eating someone else's garbage, despite my starvation. I wish I could say that not all the Germans were bastards, but they were. But occasionally, some were less bastardly than others.

Most of these Nazis were previously civilians who were menial laborers, much like the Blitz Fraus. Garbage haulers or street sweepers were turned into big shots with authority granted by the Nazi uniform. Suddenly, they were feared and had the power to hurt people with no consequences. That was how a typical Nazi was born.

As time went by at Stutthof, we were all skin and bones and lived day to day, doubtful that we would ever survive. The entire camp was filled with Jews, no gypsies or mentally ill people. Just Jews. There was so much killing happening around us that most gave up on praying to God.

However, on Yom kippur we would all still fast, not that it was difficult. It was inconceivable to me that I am in a place where there are no consequences for taking a person's life. In fact, it's rewarded.

There was no Geneva Convention or Red Cross to protect our lives. We were being murdered like vermin. Killing a group of humans was as easy as stepping on a colony of ants for the Germans.

Chapter 16

It was at the end of the summer of 1944, and after barely surviving my time at Stuthoff, and the vicious Blitz Fraus sadistic cruelty, there was a decent Aufseher who was assembling a group of women to go to a satellite camp in Bromberg, Poland. What was different about Bromberg was there were no gas chambers there. As we were lined up for roll call that morning, the Aufseher walked by and tapped us to move to the front, which meant we were chosen to leave, and were the lucky ones being sent to Bromberg. My sister and I were both young and easy choices, however my Mamma was 40 and she was bypassed and would have been left behind and probably killed. Thinking quickly, once we were "tapped," we pushed Mamma out in front of us, and snuck her into the group.

We walked to Bromberg and were surprised upon our arrival. There were no fences or barbed wire. The only security was that we were locked in our barracks at night. It was much less hostile too, although we were still guarded by Germans.

We were first put to work in a sugar beet field where we were able to steal a few beets and eat them later in our barracks. We also helped ourselves to some of the villagers' gardens we passed by on our way to the harvest fields.

One day as we were walking down the road to the fields, a stranger stopped me. He was a kind Polish man who saw me and handed me a beautiful red apple!

He could see we were emaciated and hungry, but I don't know why, out of all the women, he chose to give the apple to me.

I thanked him profusely, and I showed the apple to my sister. Her eyes lit up and she begged me for just one little bite.

Of course I was going to share the apple with my sister and Mamma, but when I handed the apple to Cyla, instead of a small bite, she took a giant bite and consumed half the apple! I was so upset with her, since it left almost nothing for me and my Mamma.

Several days later, while me and my group of women were on that same road, an elderly German man who was living in Poland approached me.

Again, I don't know why it was always me that was chosen. Maybe because I looked like I needed it the most. He was carrying a suitcase and opened it in front of me. It was full of sandwiches that he had made for us! The other women saw the food and ravaged the suitcase, and devoured all the sandwiches before I could even take one for myself. Sometimes the local citizens were empathetic and would help us, and sometimes I wasn't so lucky.

Winter came and it was bitter cold in Bromberg. I was housed with sixty other women in one room with no heat. We still had the same clothes we wore since the summer, and there were no other clothes available since no one was being killed. The malicious material the Germans chose for our outfits was designed so that, in the summer, the clothes would be hot and abrasive against our skin. In the winter, the material was ice cold like steel. Nothing was designed for our comfort, in fact it was quite the opposite.

I became severely ill during one of the worst cold snaps I had ever experienced. I was so sick, I just wanted to just stay in the freezing barrack, but no matter what, we were required to work. I dragged myself to the field with the help of my sister and Mamma, but digging frozen ground in the frigid conditions was taking its toll on me. I was desperate to the point where I spoke to the Aufseher. I told him that I was so sick and that I needed to hide in his trailer and rest or else I was going to die in the field.

He saw I wasn't going to make it, and he told me to go ahead. If he denied me I would have died out there. Rarely, could you find a German with a conscience or an ounce of kindness. I supposed I owed this Nazi my life for showing me some compassion. Our Aufseher was probably the most righteous Nazi I ever met.

As the months went on, we began hearing bombs exploding in the far distance, each day they were getting closer to our camp which meant the Russians were driving towards Germany.

I prayed that soon this might be all over, but hoped that if I were to be killed by a bomb, that it would be an American one and not a German one.

The war was coming closer to us, and the Aufseher was ordered to move us away from the bombing.

We traveled in a group, plodding on in the snow with wooden shoes on our feet.

Some nights we slept in the woods on the cold snow, and sometimes we found a dry barn to stay in. We traveled some distance when the Aufseher finally lost communication with the commandant at Stutthof.

He was frantic and complained to the Blitz Frau accompanying us that he didn't know where to go or what to do with us without direction from the Commandant.

We were inside a barn, and I intently watched and listened to them as they spoke outside the barn door.

"I lost contact with the commandant at Stuthoff and we are wandering to nowhere! The Russians will soon be upon us and I don't know what to do with my women!" exclaimed the Aufseher.

The Blitz Frau responded: "What's the problem, my friend? Throw a match and lock the barn door!" she coldly stated.

She would have had us all burned to death while locked in the barn as easily as throwing a peach pit into a garbage can.

"No! I won't do that to my women!" the Aufseher shouted at her. He gathered his things and ran off into the forest while the Blitz Frau chased after him. Suddenly in that moment, I realized that we were all alone, and FREE!!

Chapter 17

We were left all alone in the barn, and I begged my mother and sister to come with me to a farmhouse I noticed across the way. My sister refused to move.

"I'm staying put!" she exclaimed.

My Mamma was scared and stayed too. I went alone to the farm house and a Hungarian woman answered the door. It was warm in her home and she gave me some bread and water. I wanted to bring some food back for my mamma and sister, and so I returned to the barn despite wanting to stay. We all huddled together in the barn that night.

It was frightening because the war was coming closer to us. All night long, we felt and heard gunfire and bombs exploding near us. When daylight came, I got up and peeked out the barn door. Across the road was a Russian soldier standing next to his war-torn army tank.

My friend Skura and I cheerfully approached the Russian soldier. He was holding a machine gun and had a holstered pistol on his side.

"I am a Russian! Who are you?" he called out to us.

"We are Jewish girls!" we exclaimed.

"Oh! Jewish girls!" he replied, and he hugged and kissed us, and we hugged and kissed him back. He was so filthy, covered with oil and smoke from being inside the army tank. But we didn't care, he was our glorious savior!

"You girls must be hungry! Come with me and I will get you some food!" he exclaimed.

We began walking down the road with the soldier, Skura was on one side and I was on his other side, with his arms overlapping each of our shoulders. He was acting like a Russian playboy with two pretty girlfriends by his side for his comrade friends to see.

Along the way we passed a sour German man walking with an umbrella, and he gave us a look of disgust. It didn't pass the notice of the Russian soldier, and he abruptly stopped the man. He saw that the German was disgusted by his presence and he spoke to the man: "Hey, dog shit, where are you going?" He harshly questioned the man in his Russian tongue.

There was no response since the German didn't understand him, so he asked me to translate to German.

To avoid any trouble, I asked the German in a courteous way: "Where are you going, sir?"

The German squinted his face and replied to the Russian with vitriol and vulgar German terminology: "Stick your Russian head up my ass, and kiss your dog faced mother!"

I was shocked by his response, but I knew that I couldn't repeat that to the Russian soldier.

"What did he say? What did he say?" pestered the Russian.

"Uh, he says he doesn't know where he is going, and he doesn't want any trouble," I replied.

"Ohh, he doesn't know where he's going? He doesn't know?!" The Russian pulled his pistol out from its holster and pointed it at the Germans face.

He proceeded to count in German! "Eins, Zwei, Drei, Vier, Funf," and he pulled the trigger! The German's face opened up with blood, and the back of his head exploded. He fell to the ground and his bloody head landed on my feet!

"What did you do!!!" I screamed at the soldier.

"Why? Do you feel sorry for this German bastard?" he asked.

I was in shock, it all happened so fast and I didn't expect it!

But I didn't want to seem like a German sympathizer to the Russian soldier.

"No.... I don't feel sorry for him," I calmly replied.

We then continued on to a little farmhouse down the road. The Russian banged on the door with the butt of his rifle and a woman answered.

He told the woman to give us some food, but all she had was some bread. I took the bread and thanked her, and then I returned with the bread to the barn. My friend, Skura, stayed at the farmhouse with the Russian soldier and I told them I would return with my sister and Mamma.

I happily entered the barn to find them hiding in an empty horse stall. "Come out, we are free! The Germans are gone and the Russians are back! Let's go to the farmhouse where we can wash up!" I shouted to them.

My sister replied, "No, just sit. We must just sit and stay in the barn."

My sister would not move and my Mamma was satisfied staying with her. It was ridiculous that my sister was so stubborn and she refused to leave with me. I think she was in some sort of psychological shock. After being a prisoner for so long, she was afraid of our new found freedom.

I wanted to wash up, my hygiene was always important to me. So I returned to the farmhouse where Skura was still waiting for me. Our savior had left her once he was satisfied she had gotten some food. Now there was a different Russian soldier, standing with his gun ready outside the house. He spoke some friendly words and joked with me. After the night of heavy military fighting he had endured the night before, I think he was happy to be conversing with me.

I continued on and went into the farmhouse, and I asked the woman if she could give me some water to wash up.

As the woman poured water into a bowl, loud bursts of gunshots started erupting outside. "Run down into the basement!" the woman shouted.

Skura and I rushed down the stairs and the woman slammed the door closed behind us. We were down there for two minutes when suddenly we heard the farmhouse's entry door burst open.

To our horror, we once again heard ugly German voices.

"Are there any Russians here?!!" the German soldier shouted.

The woman replied: "No, just two Jewish girls in my basement."

I couldn't believe that she so quickly gave us up to the German! Immediately, he kicked the basement door open and pointed his machine gun at us. He had been killing everyone in his path, so what would it matter to kill a pair of Jews.

Fortunately, he was not a Nazi but an infantry soldier who had no interest in killing us, only Russians, and he quickly bolted away. Skura and I ran upstairs and I asked the woman if I could bring my Mamma and sister to hide there.

She replied, "No, but you and your friend can stay here."

I couldn't leave my sister and Mamma, so I left the house and headed back to the barn where they were hiding.

Just as I crossed the street, a caravan of German trucks began to pass me. They were all cheering and waving to me as if they were my heroes. I pretended to cheer them on as they drove past me, but inside, blood was pouring from my soul.

When I returned to the barn, I found three strangers lying dead outside of the barn. One was the farmer, the other two I had never seen before. The barn door was riddled with bullet holes and I held my breath as I opened the door. I feared the worst.

There I found my sister and Mamma, still hiding in a horse stall and upset because they thought I was dead! During all the shooting, a bullet had narrowly passed by them and struck a woman sitting behind them in the leg.

Suddenly my sister's demeanor changed and her face became stern. Cyla stood up and began heading for the door.

"Where are you going?" I asked.

"I'm leaving on my own. I'll never survive with you two saddled on my back!" she shouted as she left the barn.

Suddenly, I was left all alone with my Mamma and we were both in shock.

"Go after her, Rochelka! She is all mixed up and doesn't know what she is doing!" my Mamma cried.

I knew exactly what she was doing. She was doing what she always did, looking out for herself! I chased after her and grabbed onto her. I was crying and begging her not to leave us alone. She was determined to leave and fought me off as she continued down the road.

Finally I shouted, "Pappa will be angry with you when he finds out that you left us alone to save your own skin!"

She suddenly stopped; I seemed to strike a chord with her. She reluctantly turned around without speaking a word and returned to the horse stall where my Mamma was.

She was always seeking to be praised by our Pappa for doing something good, and the thought that he would be disappointed in her again, was enough to change her mind.

Now that we were back together in the barn, I once again tried to convince them to all leave together. My sister still insisted on hiding in the barn, since the three of us would obviously appear to the Germans as Jews on the run.

We lost our chance; A few hours later, we were completely surrounded by Nazis. Our moment of freedom was short-lived.

Chapter 18
The Death March

There were about seventy of us hiding in the barn when the Germans surrounded us. These were not infantry soldiers, but a band of blood thirsty Nazi SS. And so began our 30 day death march to Germany.

There was no reason for them to take us. There was no place to make us work and they were losing the war. The only reason they had was their goal to kill as many Jews before the war was over and try to cover it up.

Snow covered the ground and it was difficult to walk in the wooden shoes we were wearing. Snow would accumulate on the bottoms and they provided no traction, and we were constantly slipping and sliding. The vicious and sadistic guards were the worst any of us had ever encountered. If you showed any sign of weakness, you would be shot and killed.

They were constantly waving their guns at us and would often call out, "If anyone is tired, step out to the left and we will let you have a nice long rest!" They were killing people all around us.

We tried to stay in front of the pack since the tired Jews who couldn't keep up were gunned down in the back. Whenever we heard a gunshot from behind, we were too afraid to look back to see who they killed since that was enough for a Nazi to kill one of us.

At night, we slept in barns or on the snow. I have no idea why they just didn't finish this and kill all of us.

One morning, after weeks of marching, they were rushing us to leave a barn we had spent the night in, when I felt a single piece of straw had found its way into my wooden shoe. It was hard and sharp and was jabbing directly into the arch of my foot with each step I took. If I stopped for even a second to remove the piece of straw, they would have shot and killed me!

A raw blister developed from it, and every step I took drove the piece of straw deeper and deeper into my wound. I was trudging on in agony for hours. We were finally in a German city, and I couldn't go on. It got to a point where I couldn't take the pain anymore. I was ready to give up and let them kill me.

I cried to my Mamma and sister, "I can't go on, I can't go on!"

They both started to cry. "We won't let you die here alone! If they kill you, they will have to kill us too, we won't leave you alone to die!" my Mamma cried.

"Try to walk with us a little bit further!" my sister pleaded.

With what little strength I had left, I pushed myself on through the unbearable pain.

Luckily, a short distance later we came to a place where they gave us water to drink. It gave me the opportunity to stop and remove that menacing piece of straw that almost got me killed. Immediately, I washed my foot and wrapped paper around my blister and I began to recover.

The Nazis were distracted by the city people and were hesitant to kill anyone while outsiders were watching, even though some of the German people were heckling and bullying us.

There was a brief opportunity for the three of us to slip away and we hid behind a storage shed, but a German policeman saw us and chased us back within the group. After 30 days, half of the people we began the march with were killed.

Chapter 19
Euphoria

It seemed that the city we had arrived in was some sort of Jew distribution center. It was a cold winter morning, and the miserable Nazi SS guards herded our group to the train station where there were hundreds of other Jews like us, waiting for what was to come next.

There was a long train connected to dozens of cattle cars covered in snow. The Nazis began brutally pushing and hitting people, and occasionally shooting anyone who they had the inclination to kill. I was pushed into the cattle car by a wave of terrified people behind me. They were frightened that if they didn't get into the cars, they would be shot and killed on the train platform.

My sister and Mamma were separated from me, and I was pushed to the back of the cattle car as more and more people were stuffed in.

I don't know how much time went by, maybe an hour, but somehow I found myself just lying there on the filthy floor of the cattle car, as everyone else towered above me. I didn't know how I got there, since the last thing I remember I was standing shoulder to shoulder with everyone else.

Suddenly, as I lay there I was overwhelmed by the most beautiful feeling. A feeling of euphoria and delight came over me. I felt myself rising and then floating upward in the air, hovering above all the people that I was locked in the cattle car with.

Then something fantastic appeared before me. I saw the most beautiful beam of blue light. I felt comforted by it. I was drawn to it, and I wanted to enter it.

I entered the light, and there were more beautiful blue lights surrounding me and I was so comfortable and at peace.

I felt a loving presence embrace me, but the lights were so bright I couldn't see who it was.

Then I felt Jenya's presence, as a child's small hand took hold of mine and led me deeper into the blue lights. I felt happiness, joy and deep unconditional love! I was once again with my darling little sister, Jenya. But now, it was forever. I felt Euphoria.

At the other end of the cattle car, Cyla was frightened that she lost track of me, and was desperately looking for me in the packed cattle car.

She jumped on top of people and clawed her way over them to get to where she had seen me last.

She found me lifeless, under a pile of girls who were sitting and leaning on top of my motionless body. She fiercely pushed and dragged everyone off of my body. But she was too late. I was already dead and passing through those beautiful blue lights. I was dead, and I was happy, and with Jenya.

Cyla had some sugar wrapped in a piece of paper tucked in her pocket, which she had been saving for an emergency. She lifted my head from the floor and sprinkled the sugar into my mouth and shook me.

"Come back! Come back, Rochelka!" she screamed and continued to shake me.

Suddenly, I tasted the sweetness from the sugar and like a vacuum I was sucked back from the blue lights, my hand torn from my little sister's hand and we reached out for each other as I was pulled back. I opened my eyes. Rather than seeing Angels in heaven, I was back in the fires of hell! I was so angry with Cyla for bringing me back from my death, I started to argue and fight with my sister.

"What do you want from me! I felt so wonderful and was in the beautiful blue lights! Why did you bring me back to this hell!" I cried.

My sister held me tightly. "The sugar didn't bring you back from death. It wasn't your time to die and God sent you back," she replied.

I began to get some air and realized that maybe my sister was right, it wasn't my time to die.

Everything so far has happened for a reason and luck made it possible for us to survive.

The train began to jerk as it started rolling away from the train station. There was chatter that we were going to Falkenberg, Germany.

When the train finally stopped, we were let out and there was a firepit in the train yard that some workers had left smoldering.

My sister found a rusty tin can which she filled with snow and placed the can in the firepit. The snow quickly melted and my sister offered me and my Mamma some of the water. It was so crisp and delicious, it was the best drink of water I ever had in my life.

Shortly after, the guards got busy and moved us on. We walked a short distance until we came upon an abandoned brick factory, and they forced us inside and locked us in.

The Germans were being driven back by the Russians and they were in chaos trying to retreat and keep us captive. All we could imagine was that they brought us to the brick factory to kill all of us, but for what reason? Possibly to blow up the factory and make it appear as if an allied bomb had killed us all.

My sister and I decided that rather than sit around and wait for them to kill us, we should try to find a way out and get away. All three of us began running through the building to any door we could find. At every door we opened, there was always an armed guard standing on the other side.

Finally, we discovered a little iron coal door leading to the outside. Unfortunately, it was about ten feet above the ground, but there was no other choice in the matter.

It was our only way out. We crawled out backwards, clinging to the bottom of the doorway, and slid down the wall as far as we could before letting go.

We landed softly onto a pile of coal, but best of all we were outside and free again!

We scurried off and tried to blend in with the public. Since there were so many Germans running away, it was easier than before to slip away.

We came across a little German house and my sister knocked on the door.

"Hold your tongue and let me do all the talking," she insisted.

A nervous German woman answered the door, and my sister did her schtick: "Good afternoon, lovely lady. My name is Grace, this is my Mamma and my sister Wanda. We were kitchen workers for our glorious German infantry soldiers in Poland. Our kitchen was suddenly bombed by those dog faced

Russians, and now those terrible bastards are right on our heels. We left everything behind including our clothes. Both you and I, being German patriots and supporters of our great leader, must do our part to help one another. It would be very appreciated if you granted us some help, as we are trying to get to our home in Hamburg. Would a beautiful woman such as yourself allow my sister, mother and I to stay at your home overnight? Tomorrow we will continue running further to our home."

The woman took the bait and fawned over my sister and replied: "You poor girls, be thankful you got away with your lives, you can always buy new clothes. You can stay over for one night, but tomorrow I have German troops who will be staying here as well."

We looked at each other in bewilderment.

No matter what, we couldn't get away from these bastard Germans. Additionally, I realized what an incredible bull-shitter my sister was! She actually convinced the woman to let us into her home, and stay the night.

The house wasn't Buckingham Palace as we noticed all the floors were covered with hay.

Cyla asked the woman for some water so that I could clean the infected blister on my foot and she gave her a pail and a clean bandage to wrap my blister.

"But remember, you have to leave tomorrow," she reminded us.

We slept on her hay floor, and the following morning we left early before the soldiers might arrive.

From then on, I was called Wanda and my sister was Grace. Two very non-Jewish names to hide our identities.

We continued down the road and my sister knocked on the door of another German home further down the way, and sang the same song about working in the kitchens for the German troops and getting bombed and running away from the Russians, leaving our belongings behind.

My sister was so proficient at lying that even I began to believe her convincing stories!

We did this for an entire week, staying overnight at strangers' homes until one day my sister knocked on a door and an older German man opened the door. He listened to my sister's spiel and invited us in. He mentioned that he already had some visitors and that we couldn't stay overnight, but he had some bread for us.

We walked into his house and to our horror, it was inhabited with twelve Gestapo Nazis!

They were in their brown uniforms with big swastikas on their armbands. I almost died! They would surely recognise our outfits and know we were Jews on the run.

My sister stepped up and began flattering the men. "Oh my, what a privilege to be in a home with Hitler's finest police men, and all so handsome too!" she gushed.

My heart was pounding as my sister spoke to them, and I tried to fade into the background with my mother. They were not in the mood for flattery since they were losing the war, and were going to be hunted down for war crimes.

One of the Nazis barked at the old German man, "Why did you let these filthy peasants in here, throw them out! We have important business to discuss!"

We were quickly hustled out by the German man, and he apologized that he could not help us!

"Where can we go?" my sister asked.

The German man thought for a moment, "Why don't you go to the NFL building? It's a closed down movie theater in town. That's where all the displaced Germans are going, and they will feed you too. It's down by the train station," the German man stated.

"Oh, thank you, that's such a great idea from such a handsome man! That sounds like the perfect place for us! That's where we will go," my sister gushed.

We left the house in a hurry, just in case any of the Nazis recognised our camp uniforms. There was no way we were going to the NFL where all the Germans were congregating. We knew that there would be police there, and a good possibility we would be captured again. Once we left the house though, we noticed a young twelve year old boy, a Hitler Jungend. He was probably the son of one of those Nazis in the house.

He was following us from a distance, but keeping an eye where we were going. Most likely he realized something didn't seem right about us.

Now we had to go to the NFL, or that little Nazi punk would report us to the gestapo Nazis at the house and we would be done for! We were near the train station and saw the NFL building.

There was a policeman standing at the corner in front of the building, and the Nazi boy ran over to him. He was telling the policeman something as he was looking and pointing at us. Once again, I thought that we were found out and going to be recaptured, all because that little Nazi had it out for us! All we could do was be calm and enter the NFL building, just like all the other German refugees. We felt as if we were lambs entering a lion's den!

Once we entered, we found out they were offering loaves of bread and coffee to all the refugees. I watched my sister take a loaf of bread, then oddly walk back towards the building entrance. She went outside where the policeman was standing and began flirting with him! I thought she was crazy!!

"Are you hungry, officer? I have so much bread, and I can share some with you!" she stated in her kiss-ass voice.

"No girl, I'm not hungry. But thank you for your concern," and he laughed.

She then returned, back into the NFL building with the bread, smiling.

"Are you crazy? Why did you go to the policeman with the bread?" I exclaimed.

"I didn't want him to think we were hiding something." She shrugged.

"I don't think he was coming after us, that was stupid and risky," I replied.

"I'll bring this bread to Mamma. Go into the other room and fill up the coffee pot," she rudely ordered.

I shook my head in disgust, and walked across to the room where the coffee was being served. I entered the room and an elderly German woman filled my pot, and I thanked her.

As I left the room carrying the hot coffee pot, there in the doorway was the German policeman who chased us out of our hiding place at the train station! He was standing right in front of me! He locked onto me with his ice cold stare.

"Wait, you are familiar to me! I know you! I saw you from someplace!" he proclaimed with his finger up in the air.

My heart sank, but I learned something from my sister: how to be a good liar.

"I'm sorry officer, we've never met. Certainly I would remember a handsome man such as yourself. You have made a mistake," I confidently stated and walked away with my pot of coffee.

He was watching me, and rather than go to where my Mamma and sister were, I went to the opposite corner of the cinema. If he suddenly remembered, he would only take me. If he saw us together he would definitely remember all of us.

I decided that we had been in the area much too long and were already known by too many Germans. We had to get out of Falkenberg, as soon as possible.

In the meantime, the policeman was called away, and my sister had found an old dress that someone left behind. It was important that she could change into it, so at least we weren't all dressed the same, and wouldn't stand out.

Chapter 20

We began walking away from town heading east towards Poland. The Germans were being pushed farther back from the fronts.

We were hungry, our clothes were filthy and we were so tired.

We finally came to a small town and went to an employment office. My sister told the female agent the same story about us being kitchen workers for the German soldiers. By now she really had that story fine-tuned and polished. Cyla was such a good liar, the employment agent believed my sister.

"We are tired from running away from those terrible Russians. Can you find us a job on a farm?" my sister questioned.

The agent sent us to a nearby village, where my sister and mamma worked at a farm milking cows and cleaning animal waste. I got a job working in a farm house peeling potatoes, cleaning and doing laundry.

They liked me, and the farmer gave me a beautiful blanket.

I was there a short time when they suspected something was wrong with me. I could not stop scratching my head. They brought in a nurse to look me over, and she found lice in my hair. I was immediately fired. I offered to shave my head, but the Germans were so paranoid about germs and uncleanliness that I had to leave.

I had no place to go but to the farm where my sister and mamma worked. I cried and told Cyla I was fired because they found lice in my hair. She hid me under the covers of her bed and snuck me cooked potatoes that were meant for the pigs. Soon after, my sister, who wasn't very good with animals, was fired as well. The three of us were on the run again.

We were lucky to find another employment office. While we were there waiting, a man pulled up with a horse and buggy and asked us if we were looking for work in exchange for food.

We agreed, and he took the three of us to work on his farm.

There were people in Germany that were once Polish and they changed their citizenship to German when Poland was invaded. They called them Eingedeutched (Turned to German).

They were very much hated by the Polish and Russian soldiers that were closing in on the Germans. The fact that they traded their born heritage to become Germans didn't sit well with true Polish patriots. We were telling people to cover our Jewish heritage that we were Eingedeutched as well, and we became German citizens.

When the farmer brought us to his home, his wife made a wonderful dinner for us.

There was fish and potatoes, with some bread. Since this was our first dinner together, the farmer insisted that I be the first to serve myself and he handed me a plate. The food looked so delicious and we hadn't eaten a real meal since before the war.

I took a piece of fish and a potato.

I watched as the farmer took only a piece of fish and no potato.

I panicked! "Why did I take a potato! I should have only taken a piece of fish, as the farmer did! They are going to find out about me!"

I was so conditioned by the Germans to believe that everything I did could get me into trouble. Even after we were free, I still feared being punished for anything I did.

After supper, the wife went to bed and I cleaned up. I was still very hungry and there was a pantry room off the kitchen.

I went in there and stuffed my face with food she had prepared for the pigs.

The following morning, I told her that I had lost all my clothes running from the Russians. She had a daughter and she gave me some of her clothes to wear. I was beginning to feel human again.

As the days passed the farmer's wife became more comfortable with me. One night she and I were sitting by the fireplace and she said, "Wanda, you know we have a black end."

"We what?" I replied as we watched the fire dance and the embers glowed.

"We (the Germans) killed so many innocent Jews," she matter-of-factly stated.

I was silent because I didn't know what to do: Faint, cry, or scream. But tears began to pour from my eyes. She had just confessed to me that the German citizens did, in fact, know what was happening to the Jews. They stayed silent and were complacent despite knowing about the murdering of Jews in the concentration camps.

The following day, German trucks filled with war-torn soldiers began retreating down the road past the farmer's home.

The farmer's wife, who was still patriotic, compassionately asked me to go give "our" soldiers water to drink because they were thirsty.

I wanted to give them poison, not water, but I had to play my role as a Polish German. So we brought them water. The German soldiers were begging us to hop onto the trucks and run off with them!

"Girls, girls, come with us! The Russians are coming and we will save you! We'll take care of you! Come with us!" they shouted.

They made me sick and I said under my breath: "Yeah, yeah, you will go to hell you sons of bitches... choke on this water!"

That evening, this time the farmer spoke to me as we once again sat by the fireplace.

"Wanda, the Russian and Polish soldiers are coming shortly. Are you afraid? They hate the Poles that became German citizens, and they might kill you if they find out you are Eingedeutched."

We were so good at concealing our identity, he couldn't even imagine that I was a Jew.

"Oh, you're crazy!" I joked. But in fact it was true, the Polish and Russian soldiers were coming, and the Germans were fleeing like pigs from a butcher's cleaver.

The Germans and Eingedeutched knew that once the Russians and Polish soldiers arrived, they were done for, so they were running off.

The following morning, an Eingedeutched man dressed in plain clothes wandered into the farm with his little girl by his side. The farmer's wife nudged me when she saw him, and he was known to her.

She whispered to me, "He must be scared, he is a Nazi!"

I was wary of him and he seemed intense, like he had something to hide.

A few minutes later, we heard the rumble of military vehicles coming down the road towards us. There were Russian tanks and other military vehicles along with soldiers on foot. A wild-eyed Polish soldier entered the yard and approached me.

"Are you a Jew?" he questioned.

I looked at him and my heart sank.

I thought, "Is this what I survived for? To die by the hand of my enemy's enemy, our savior?" It was my reflex reaction to always deny that we were Jews, so I responded, "Are you crazy? They killed all the Jews a long time ago."

"If you're not a Jew then say a Christian prayer," he ordered.

My Christian friend, Yajah, was with me and she intervened, "Are you a real Polski? Of course we can pray, what Polish girl can't pray?" Suddenly, something clicked in my head and I began singing Silent Night, from my memory of Christmas Eve with Wanda. The soldier was satisfied.

I'm not sure what he would have done if he learned I was a Jew, but he knew I was Polish and not a German.

He quickly turned his attention to the Nazi and his daughter. "Who is this guy? I'll kill him like a dog if he's a Nazi!" the soldier shouted at me in Polish.

The Nazi understood exactly what the soldier was asking of me, and he stared at me with his evil Nazi eyes. I looked at him and he looked at me, not knowing that I knew his secret.

His daughter was my little sister's age. In my heart I screamed, "Kill this son of a bitch Nazi bastard!" but from my mouth came, "I don't know who he is."

The soldier ran off and the Nazi tipped his hat and smirked at me. Suddenly, I was overwhelmed with a feeling of guilt that would haunt me for the rest of my life, along with me putting my little sister on the train to her death.

What was wrong with me?

Why didn't I let that soldier kill that piece of human waste!

I couldn't, I just couldn't say it! After what those stone-hearted, sadistic animals did to my family, my little sister and my people!

How could I not kill one single Nazi when I had the chance! I am a worthless Jew.

Chapter 21

I ran to my sister who was walking down the street towards me. I decided that we couldn't stay here anymore.

We need to get far away from these Germans, and we need to head back to Poland.

"Let's get out of here, let's get out of here now!" I commanded.

"It's no good to leave now, remember we were free once and we got caught again by the Germans!" Cyla exclaimed.

"It's different now, tomorrow morning we are leaving! It's too dangerous for us here!" I was so insistent that she finally agreed with me.

We began walking back to the farmhouse when we came across three Polish soldiers.

They were standing together and I noticed one of the soldiers was oddly squeezing his pimples on his face. As we walked by them, I casually said to the soldier "Don't kvetch," which is a Yiddish word for squeeze. He looked at me startled, and my sister almost killed me for saying a Yiddish word.

The soldier lit up! "Are you a Jew? I'm a Jew too!"

We were afraid and we ran away from him, but he chased after me. I was so scared! He grabbed me and shouted, "Tell me! Are you Jewish?"

My sister was making angry faces at me to keep quiet! He was begging me to tell him, since he was so desperate to find a living Jew, after so many millions were slaughtered and almost extinct.

But I replied, "No, I'm not Jewish."

He could tell I was hiding it, and maybe he felt that I didn't like him. He sadly backed off.

"I'm sorry, please excuse me," he stated with disappointment.

I went back to the farm, crying. Why didn't I tell him? I was so upset with myself, but after 5 years of being a prisoner, it was difficult to trust anyone. Especially admitting that I was a Jew.

The following morning it was time to go.

The farmer's dog, Katzel (which ironically means kitten), was attached to me. He followed me wherever I would go, and so the farmer held him tightly when I left.

There was a migration of Polish people returning to Poland and there were a few at the farm who were also leaving with us.

One had a horse and cart which they allowed my mamma to ride in with them. Cyla and I walked along with my friend Yajah. We were all going back to Poland.

There were Russian and Polish soldiers everywhere and it was chaos! People who worked on the farms were killing each other, and the soldiers were carrying guns and robbing the German citizens.

As we began traveling, a Russian soldier on a bicycle passed by us then turned back. He began walking with us, and he introduced himself as Vladimir. He shook my sister's hand, he then shook Yajah's hand, and then shook my hand. However, he would not let go of me.

"What's your name, Beautiful?" he asked as he held my hand tightly.

"My name is Wanda. It is nice to meet you, but you're hurting my hand and I have to go!" I nervously replied.

"Wanda, such a beautiful name. Come with me, Wanda!" he begged.

When my sister and Yadja tried to interrupt and get me away from him, he pulled his gun and chased them away! He wouldn't let me go and he tightened his grip on my hand.

Cyla tried to get between us and break his grip!

"Wanda, Wanda, come along!" my sister exclaimed.

The Russian became severely agitated and he pushed Cyla out of the way and he wildly shouted: "Get away from us! Or l will kill you all!"

I begged him to let me go and I screamed for help!

People were traveling by and shouting, "Leave the little girl alone, she's just a child!" But no one stopped to help me.

Katzel, the farm dog, saw that I was in distress and was barking wildly.

He broke away from the farmer and came racing up the road from behind us, and he viciously attacked the Russian soldier!

The Russian dropped his bicycle and I pulled away from him. I ran away and jumped into the cart my mamma was in and I hid!

There was a loud tumult of the dog fighting, and the soldier screaming in agony.

Then I heard a gunshot, and the dog was silenced.

The Russian was bloody and wounded and his clothes ripped apart, but he wasn't lazy. He picked up his bicycle and chased after me.

He stopped the wagon and shouted at me, "If you don't come down and go with me, I will kill you right here!"

A Polish girl who was riding in the wagon said, "Wanda, why don't you just go with him? Go ahead already!"

"Why don't *you* go with him!" I harshly replied. I then covered my face with my hands and I cried.

Everyone was begging the Russian to leave me alone. He raised his rifle and pointed it at me! "You would rather be dead like your dog than come with me? You piece of Polish garbage."

"Yes! I would rather be dead! I'm not going with you! Kill me! Kill me! I'm a child! I won't go with you!" I cried and my mother started to cry!

If my Pappa were here he would handle this piece of Russian trash his way, but we had lost track of his whereabouts a year ago.

The Russian was wild-eyed and continued calling me all sorts of terrible names when my sister noticed two big Polish soldiers walking past her. Cyla clung to them and begged them to help me.

"Handsome friends, please take this Russian away from us. He is trying to abduct my little sister and she is only a child!" she pleaded with them. The two soldiers stopped and saw what was happening.

They approached the Russian and humorously chatted with him.

"Comrade, what do you want from this child? Come with us and we will bring you to a real German whore. You will get what you want and she will eagerly do it for you!"

"No, I want this girl!" he raged on, and he continued swearing at me.

The other Polish soldier responded, "Come with us my communist friend, you obviously need some vodka to soothe your soul!"

They each tucked their arms under his armpits and dragged him away with them. The whole time he kept turning back and continued swearing vicious words at me. He would have killed me if it wasn't for those Polish soldiers.

Superstitious people were saying that the dog had sacrificed his life in my place. I felt sad for Katzel. He loved me and wanted to protect me. Maybe he did give up his life for me.

Chapter 22

We continued on with the caravan. It was a slow journey and we weren't sure where we were going. But we were sure of one thing: the farther away we could get from Germany the better.

Later that same day, another soldier on a bicycle passed us by.

Of all the hundreds of people in the caravan he immediately stopped next to me and my sister.

I was scared because the last time a soldier on a bicycle stopped next to me, there was big trouble.

This young soldier spoke to me in a kind way. "I am a Jew. Are you girls Jewish?" he hopefully asked.

My sister gave me a stern look again, to say no.

"No, no we're not Jewish. They killed all the Jews around here," I replied.

The soldier looked puzzled and drove off on his bicycle. But he was bothered and circled back, and he approached me once again. "I'm sorry to bother you, but you are a shana madel (pretty girl in Yiddish) and you're a real Jewish type. Aren't you Jewish?" he softly questioned.

When I heard him speak Yiddish I couldn't hold it in any longer, despite my sister squeezing my arm!

"Yes we are Jews!" I grabbed him and kissed him and hugged him and together we cried!

It was such a relief to tell someone that I was a Jew! He asked us where we were going. We really had no idea except to regroup in Poland and search for my Pappa.

"Go back to Bromberg," he instructed.

"There is a hospital with Jewish girls working there. They will help you!"

We parted ways and headed back to Bromberg, the town where we were previously imprisoned.

Once we arrived at the hospital, the girls helped us get jobs. My Mamma and Cyla were working in the hospital and I got a job in a dentist's office. We couldn't stay in Poland; there was nothing for us there. Our families were gone and we had nothing.

We decided it was best to migrate to a survivors camp in Berlin, where I was determined to find my Pappa.

Sadly, once we arrived in the refugee camp, I found a survivor named Yostel who was with my Pappa during the final days of the war.

He held my hands and solemnly spoke to me: "The Nazis, until the very end, were determined to kill as many Jews as possible. Hundreds, maybe thousands of Jews at Stutthof were marched into the sea and mowed down with machine guns. They began transporting large groups of Jews out of the area in ships over the Baltic Sea. Your father was a friend of mine, and we were together on one of those ships.

"He was very sad to be away from you and his family. He asked everyone he met, 'Did you happen to see the most beautiful girl in the camps? That would be my daughter, Rochelka! And if you see her, tell her I love her so much, and I will meet her in Vienna.' You were very special to your Pappa, and he lit up whenever he spoke of you. You made him very proud.

"One night on the ship, I saw that he was very quiet and sad. He told me he was going for a walk, and that someone special who was all alone, was waiting for him.

"He never returned.

"That was the last anyone saw of him.

"A few hours later, the Nazi's forced everyone on the deck into the ocean and they all drowned at sea. He must have been on the deck when that happened. I was below and survived."

My eyes were full of tears and I knew he was determined to be with Jenya.

I am not selfish and understood his need to be with her. I hope and pray they are both together now, and that they are at peace in the bright blue lights of heaven.

I thanked the man for telling me what happened. I sadly returned to our place in the refugee camp and broke the sad news to my Mamma and Cyla. It was inevitable, Pappa was so heartbroken and he didn't want Jenya to be alone. All that we had left now was each other.

The survivors' refugee camp was a place for families and loved ones who were lost to possibly be reunited.

We thought that we were the only Jews left in Europe, since all of us had lost numerous family members. Men and women were gravitating to each other quickly. My sister met a Jewish Polish soldier, Simon Wilensky, and was married after only a week! Men who lost their wives were becoming couples with women who lost their husbands. Who knew if love had anything to do with it. There was a common thread everyone shared: they survived and love might follow.

I met my husband, Jorek Blocher, in the survivors camp.

He had lost his mother Esther, his wife Zlota and his two young children. Katriel, who was 5, and Sarah, who was only 2 years old.

They were all attacked and slaughtered by Lithuanian butchers working for the Nazis.

He narrowly escaped and was hidden by two Polish farmers who risked their lives to conceal him. He was much older than me (thirteen years) and I was apprehensive about him since he was much more mature, and a wheeler and dealer in the refugee camp.

As an engagement gift, he had given me a small golden Angel pin to wear. Sadly, hours after he gave it to me, the pin unclasped and I lost it somewhere in the refugee camp.

I was upset and it was already dark when I told him that I lost the golden Angel.

He asked me where I had walked, and he took a lantern and went looking for the angel.

About an hour later he returned and was excited to reveal that he had found the golden Angel laying in the dirt where many people had been walking.

It was lucky and it was a miracle that he was able to find it, and I always treasured it. Once again luck was on my side.

I still wasn't sure about marrying him, however my sister and mamma convinced me he was a good man and we were married six months after we met. We had a small wedding under a chuppah where a Rabbi performed the ceremony. There were no fancy wedding clothes, and only my family and our friends attended.

Shortly after our papers were finally cleared to allow us entry into America.

My dream of going to America was coming true.

We left August 16, 1946 on the ship SS Marine Marlin.

My husband disappeared for several days during the voyage. I was very concerned and I feared he jumped off the ship!

When he finally reappeared, green and deathly ill, he stated, "Had I known the curse of sea sickness, I would have stayed in Berlin with those German bastards!"

When we finally arrived in New York, it was amazing as the ship pulled into New York harbor where we saw the glorious Statue of Liberty, with her flaming torch held high!

It was extremely emotional for us and we were all crying.

For the first time in a long time, we felt safe again.

My husband had friends and relatives in New York City, and unbeknownst to them, he had accumulated a small fortune trading for gold and platinum with the German citizens whose money turned out to be worthless after the war ended.

Before we left Germany, he actually bought a house in Eastern Germany for the cost of a box of matches!

I asked him why he needed it since we were leaving. He replied, "The owner was a devout German woman and a Jew hater. It gave me satisfaction that a Jew bought her home for the price of a box of matches. Besides, it was so cheap I couldn't resist!"

My sister Cyla and her husband migrated to Vineland, New Jersey where they started a chicken farming business. My Mamma chose to stay with me in New York.

With the help of my husband's relatives in Connecticut, on May 6, 1948 he was able to find and purchase a functioning dairy farm in Southington,

Connecticut, cashing in platinum bars that he had brought with him (which he had swindled from the Russians. But that's another story). The farm included 150 acres of land, 40 cows, two tractors, some farm equipment and a 250 year-old house that once belonged to a civil war captain.

The house had no heat, no hot water, no electricity, no refrigerator, and we had no transportation.

It was almost as bad as the camps! All we had was a wood stove. My daughter Esther (named after Jorek's mother) was born just two weeks after we arrived there.

The following year, our first son Gerald (Yuruchim) was born and named after my beloved father.

Through hard work and determination, from selling milk and eggs and some lucky breaks, we soon had enough money to renovate our home.

We acquired all the amenities we were missing and even bought the first dishwasher ever sold in our town. Five years later, my son William was born and five years after that my youngest son, Barry.

Despite the insurmountable joy and happiness my family brought to me, I still carry a black hole inside my heart and soul from what the Germans and their collaborators did to us.

I have dreams of the horrific events that I saw and experienced. My dreams though, are of a different sort.

Most people wake up from a bad dream and the dream is over. For me, when I wake up and fall back asleep, my horrific dreams continue where they left off.

Often I wake up screaming.

Screaming for my little sister Jenya and my Pappa to come back to me!

Other times, I scream for my people who were senselessly and sadistically murdered.

I scream for the babies that had their skulls cracked and then tossed into the back of garbage trucks, and their mothers who fought with all their might to protect their children.

I scream for the victims, both children and adults, who were buried alive and suffocated under the dirt because they weren't worth a Nazi's Bullet.

I scream, because the world knew what was happening to us and no one cared.

I scream because I saw for myself, how civilized people could be brainwashed to hate someone, and become so sadistically cruel with no empathy towards another human being's life.

I scream for the victims and women who were murdered in the death march whose only crime was that their hair was frozen to the ground and they were shot in the head for not being able to get up.

And I scream for all the victims of Hitler's gas chambers and the children who were tortured and murdered.

Now I'm considered a Holocaust survivor. If surviving means that I lived through it physically, then I suppose that I am a survivor.

But the emotional scars that haunt me, I don't believe I can ever heal from that.

As a young girl my only hopes and dreams were growing up in a kind hearted world, reading magical books, becoming a famous piano player, marrying a prince, watching movies at the cinema with my friends and being with my little sister, Jenya forever, because I love her so much.

And possibly finding two snowflakes that are exactly alike!

On September 11, 2004, I once again rose from the floor of that cattle car only this time it was a hospital bed, and I divinely passed through those glorious blue lights once again. This time it was God's will and my journey was now complete. I was happy and felt at peace again. My little sister was waiting for me and she embraced me and told me not to be afraid. I was so happy to feel her warmth and her soft face against my cheek.

She led me deeper into the blue lights where my Pappa, Mamma and Cyla were waiting for me. I never found two snowflakes that were exactly alike…. But I am grateful to be with my little sister, Jenya and my family forever.

Afterword

Approximately a week before my mother passed away from cancer, the oncologists were diligently trying to prolong my mother's life. It came to the point where my mother was doped up and unconscious on drugs and in pain. It was when the Oncologist ordered another CT scan to determine how much her cancer progressed that week that we realized she had had enough.

I reflected back on the story she had often told me about how she had died in the cattle car and she felt so good and was finally at peace. She was angry with her sister for bringing her back to hell. No matter what the doctors were telling me, that she could come out of this and live a little longer, I felt that it was temporary and she would only relive this torture another day in the near future.

Based entirely on what she went through, dying that day in the cattle car, prompted me to make the hardest decision of my life…to let her go. I believe with all my heart that's what she wanted. She was ready now to pass through the magnificent blue lights, and she could finally feel euphoria and once again be reunited with her family that she missed and loved so much.

www.ingramcontent.com/pod-product-compliance
Lightning Source LLC
Chambersburg PA
CBHW030554080526
44585CB00012B/372